THE CREATIVE WILD

It's so encouraging to read an author working in the faith/arts/creativity space who writes with such clarity about the essentials of creativity. I was especially enthused/relieved to see that risk made it into this book—an absolute essential to making a song, a business, or a life. "Risk or rust," is what I once heard a friend say. Wise words. As is this entire book. A point of clarification, though: Read this book if you want to live a 24/7 imaginative and creative life. It's not just for artists. This book points the way to being human in the truest sense. Who doesn't need that?

— CHARLIE PEACOCK, Grammy Award-winning music producer and author of *Roots & Rhythm—A Life in Music* and coauthor of *Why Everything That Doesn't Matter, Matters So Much*

I couldn't put down The Creative Wild *as it spoke to a deep space within me, within all of us as creative beings. This book serves as a practical guide to navigate the messiness of creativity, offering tools and strategies to break through blocks and rediscover the joy of creating. With a refreshing integration of faith and grace, it renews our sense of confidence and encourages us to embrace the unpredictable journey of artistic expression."*

— LIDIA LAE, PhD, writer, psychologist, speaker

"Creative work is fraught with insecurity and worry," Steve Brock writes. For me, it's also fraught with a nagging sense that perhaps my time is better spent on tasks that make money or produce visible progress. So many voices urge me to produce more and to do so more efficiently. When I listen to them, creating feels like an indulgence that is less important than other demands. But then I read The Creative Wild. Steve Brock convinces me that it's not just the poets and painters who are creatives. I am too. And so are you. No wonder I feel a little more human when I take time to create.

— COLLEEN HIGGS, writer

Steve Brock has helped me realize that since we're created in the image of our Creator God, then when I'm not creating, something vital in my life is missing.

— ROBERT LACHANCE, entrepreneur

The Creative Wild *invites us into a posture many of us have forgotten, a willingness to be surprised. Steve Brock lays out maps, tools, and rich stories for the journey. This call to creation comes with a cost, and this is what the book illuminates so well; it's worth every penny.*

— **CODY F. MILLER, mixed media artist**

The Creative Wild *is written so well. It is both deeply thought-provoking and entirely practical. Several times while reading the book, I had to pause for a minute to contemplate another profound insight into the creative process, especially how God works with us while we create. The Creative Wild is also immediately applicable, with scores of tools and pathways to help with obstacles to production, always in a joyful and encouraging manner.*

— **PAT SCHANTZ, writer and President of the Northwest Christian Writers Association**

The Creative Wild *is a beautiful and brilliant antidote for every believer who thinks they are ordinary, uncreative, or just plain stuck. With so many practical take-aways, like Doses and Dives and the reminder that friction is part of the process, this is a book that I will return to over and over again. Once again, Steve Brock, you have created a worthy gem.*

— **KAY EDWARDS, author of Hunt With Your Pack**

Whether you need encouragement, motivation, or a kind fellow traveler on your artistic journey, The Creative Wild *is the book for you. Steve Brock has written a book that is equal parts inspiration, practical advice, and hands-on exercises and reflections to help empower you to accomplish the art you've been called to create.*

— **MATT MIKALATOS, author of The Crescent Stone and Journey to Love**

THE CREATIVE WILD

GET UNSTUCK, CREATE MORE ADVENTUROUSLY

By Steve Brock

Copyright © 2025 by Steve Brock

All rights reserved. This book or parts thereof may not be reproduced in any form, stored in any retrieval system, or transmitted in any form by any means—electronic, mechanical, photocopy, recording, or otherwise—without prior written permission of the publisher, except as provided by United States of America copyright law. For permission requests, write to the publisher, at "Attention: Permissions Coordinator," at the following address:

Sublimity Press
300 Lenora Street # 844
Seattle, WA 98121

ISBN: 9781735118840
Library of Congress Control Number: 2024915154

All photographs are by Steve Brock
Cover and book design by Soundness Design

Printed in the United States of America

First printing edition 2025

To find out about group, corporate and private-label sales of this book contact info@sublimitypress.com

1. Creativity, 2. Spiritual Growth, 3. Christian Living

CONTENTS

INTRODUCTION 1

PART I: SPIRITUAL FOUNDATIONS FOR CREATING ADVENTUROUSLY

1. IDENTITY, CALLING, AND GRACE 11
2. STUCKNESS, ABIDING, AND CREATING AS AN ACT OF GRACE ... 19
3. CREATING ADVENTUROUSLY 26

PART II: ESSENTIALS FOR CREATING ADVENTUROUSLY

4. MINDSET, MASTERY, AND MOTIVATION 34
5. ENVIRONMENT 45
6. NAVIGATING THE CREATIVE WILD 53

PART III: TOOLS FOR CREATING ADVENTUROUSLY

7. READINESS 64
8. RHYTHM 76
9. RE-CREATION 88
10. DISCOVERY 100
11. MOVEMENT 112
12. PERSPECTIVE 124
13. PLACE 135
14. OTHERS 147
15. INDIRECTION 158
16. INCOMPLETION 170
17. RIGHTNESS 181
18. NEXT STEPS 192

APPENDIX: THE CREATIVE WILD QUESTIONS 201
ENDNOTES 206
ACKNOWLEDGMENTS 213

INTRODUCTION

Where you learn what The Creative Wild is, why you belong here, the reasons for writing this book, and what's to come.

Creating is not extraordinary, even if its results sometimes are. Creation is human. It is all of us. It is everybody.

— Kevin Ashton, ***How to Fly a Horse***

You've likely heard the story of the little kid tasked with cleaning out a very dirty stable. When asked why he scooped out the mountain of manure with such joy and enthusiasm, the kid replied, "Because there's gotta be a pony in here somewhere!"

Cute story. But what you may not have realized is this: You're the little kid.

And that pile of manure, well, that's your creative idea. Bear with me.

See if this doesn't sound familiar.

You have an idea for a new creative product. A book. A painting. A new recipe, tattoo, board game, cure, or business. Whatever it is, you're excited about it.

You spend more time dreaming of it. Jotting down additional details. Working out your Oscar or Nobel acceptance speech. Figuring out some witty retort for your interview on *The Today Show*.

And then you start the work. It goes something like this over days, weeks, months, maybe even years:

"This is garbage."

"This is garbage."

"This is garbage."

"Wait. This could be… Nope. This is garbage."

"What made me think I could do this?"

"I have a new idea that will change all this!"

"Not bad. Not bad."

"Nope. This is garbage."

"I should start over."

"I should just give up."

"Didn't people tell me the idea was good? C'mon. Stick to it! You can do it."

"Nope. This is garbage."

"Wait. What is that? Is that a hoof?"

"Is that a pony's tail?"

"This looks like a pony. Kind of."

Refine.

Refine.

Periodic bouts of impostor syndrome.

Refine.

The sheer panic of an approaching deadline.

The motivation of the deadline to overcome those nagging perfectionist tendencies.

"This isn't bad."

Refine.

Refine.

"What do you think?" you ask a trusted colleague.

Refine.

Refine.

And then one day, you take the near-final product, and you ask another trusted friend (who knows your area, medium, genre and shares your tastes). They look at it, read through it, listen to it, etc.

And then they look at you.

Then back at the work.

Then back to you.

They say nothing, but you realize they have tears in their eyes. You say nothing, fearful those tears mean they are empathizing with you for wasting the last two years of your life on this thing.

And then they smile and say three small yet mighty words.

"This is beautiful."

They've found your pony. And so have you.

WELCOME TO THE CREATIVE WILD

Let's change the metaphor since "horse poop" and "beautiful" have likely never coexisted in the same sentence before this one.

To make something new, useful, or even beautiful, you'll need to enter what I call "The Creative Wild." As the name implies, it's an untamed place. Picture a vast forest filled with endless trees, occasional meadows, rivers, waterfalls, and rocky cliffs. It doesn't have street signs—or even streets. There are paths, but you may not know which one goes where. It is a place of wonder, mystery, beauty, and, often, the scary unknown.

I like this metaphor of a forest, but you can come up with whatever one works for you—a jungle, desert, old castle, ocean depths, complex urban environment, or overflowing closet. Any place you can picture that has elements of mystery, wonder, intrigue, and anticipation (so maybe the closet is out) will work. It's the concept that matters more than the analogy.

Everyone who has ever created has experienced The Creative Wild. It's where we go when we make things or even dream about what might be. It can be as tame as a sunny glade or as rampaging as a storm. It invites us and terrifies us. It is less an imaginary place and more a place of the imagination. A place of curiosity and inspiration and all the elements you associate with creativity. And many, you might not. It is the mental, emotional, and even spiritual space you enter—much like a studio, atelier, or workspace—when you desire to make something new. It's a figurative place, just like your happy place, only bigger, better, and with a much cooler name.

Some of you, however, may not think it's a place you belong. You may do many creative things without considering those efforts creative. Planning a meal, organizing a classroom, conducting a meeting—these and so many other everyday tasks get classified as that: everyday tasks. Not creative, and definitely not artistic or innovative.

The problem isn't with your creative abilities. It's with your labels and classifications. Creativity comes in two general forms: compositional and improvisational. And yet, most people only consider the former when thinking of their own creativity. If they've never written a book, composed a song, penned a sonnet, painted a picture, or any one of a million other examples of compositional creativity, they don't think of themselves as creative. They don't consider that coming up with a new recipe, figuring out how to motivate a co-worker, or devising a new way to sort the laundry are all forms of creativity, just the improvisational kind.

Most people don't grasp that because we are all created in the image of our Creator, each of us bears in the fiber of our being, both the ability to create and the drive to do so. But you're not "most people." You wouldn't be reading this if you didn't have at least a glimmer of hope that you have some creative abilities. Indeed, you do. In the following pages, you'll discover just how many. You just may have not yet realized or embraced that. But keep reading. You will.

For the rest of you, if you already have some sense of your creative potential, the way you navigate The Creative Wild—I mean truly thrive there and make it work for you as opposed to looking in from the perimeter—is to learn how to create adventurously. And how you do that is what this book is about. In fact, the goal of this book is to ease you into—or help you grow in—your identity as an adventurous creative. Someone who longs to do something exciting, something that matters. Who grows in wisdom and grace.

Helps others. Makes something beautiful. Glorifies God. Someone who becomes the creator your Creator Father created you to be.

The Creative Wild will be a new place for some and feel quite familiar to others. But no matter how long you've been in this world of creativity, The Creative Wild will always retain elements of mystery, even as you gain mastery navigating it. It bridges many spheres, from art to science to commerce, from individual self-expression to group or even communal action, all aimed at bringing something valuable into the world: a work of visual or written art, an innovative product or a new way of doing business, a symphonic movement or a social one.

KEY QUESTIONS WE'LL EXPLORE

In your journey through The Creative Wild, you'll likely have many questions. Here are just a few of the ones we'll explore together:

- What if, as we saw earlier, I don't think of myself as creative?
- How does my creative work relate to my sense of identity, meaning, purpose, and belonging?
- Where do I start if I'm a beginner in this world of creativity?
- How do I finish or know if my work is any good?
- What difference does believing in Jesus make to my creativity and vice versa?
- How can I make a living doing the creative work I love, or at least sell more of what I make?
- How do I overcome ruts, stuckness, impostor syndrome, and all the other forms of anxiety that pop up around creating?
- How can I make something beautiful or useful that makes a difference to others and for God's Kingdom?

Do any of these questions sound familiar? Likely so, because as we'll see, while creative people all seem to be wildly (get it?) different, we also share similar traits and interests. And when you add in the element of faith, you find our commonalities run both wide and very, very deep.

MY CREATIVE BACKGROUND

Since I'll be your guide through these questions, their answers, and so much more about The Creative Wild, let me give you an introduction.

I spent the first part of my life thinking you had to have a lot of talent to create and the last part (so far) discovering that the most creative people I know simply work harder than the rest of us. I've led a branding and marketing agency for the last 25 years, working with many of the nation's top corporations and ministries. That impresses people in corporations and ministries but earns me minimal cred with my artist friends. They see it all as business and thus not as creative as pure art. Until they realize they need branding and marketing to help them sell that pure art. Suddenly, my star rises. Kind of. I balance all this with other creative pursuits, from writing to photography, from woodworking to cooking, and from sketching to composing music that you'll learn more about in short photo essays sandwiched between the chapters in Part III.

Because of these diverse passions, I have created in many kinds of media and contexts, some for pay, some not. That gives me enough sense to empathize with both experienced professional creatives who live by deadlines and commissions, and those who may only "dabble," but for whom their creative work means everything. I understand the need for innovation in businesses who want to make a profit and can still relate to artists who resist any commercialization of their work. I've found that creative individuals exist in all fields because almost everything you use or appreciate in life results from a creative effort. That intersection of multiple areas of creativity undergirds much of this book.

So too does a deep appreciation for the wonder of making. It's a feeling of inarticulate awe I've known ever since I was a child. You've likely experienced it as well, that inexpressible delight not just in the thing you're creating, or even in the process, but in the very thought of engaging in both. Much like the bliss you derive when anticipating an upcoming trip or pleasant event, there's a joy in the dreaming of what you'll make or are making. Particularly when you're young, there's an innocent pleasure in savoring the very idea of creating. It's akin to the similar happiness that comes from merely caressing your materials, gawking at your tools, or contemplating the time you'll spend essentially playing while you make something new.

When I was small, I loved the imaginative play of taking a toy from a cereal box and using it in a Rube Goldberg-like contraption to catch a passing bug (which, alas, never passed that way). Or marveling, in an age of cheap plastic toys, over the precise metal wheels and gears of my first N scale model railroad set and repurposing parts of one train car to make a mini roller coaster. Or forming mountains, carving out riverbeds, making miniature trees, trellises, and towns, and other aspects of crafting scenery as part of that railroad. I didn't realize it then, but I was engaging in a kind of world building—even on a micro scale—that became part of so many creative efforts later, from storytelling to interior design.

Around the age of 11, I got my first magic trick. Sure, it was fun to amaze my family and friends, but even more fascinating was the intricacy of the props, both those the audience sees and the secret parts they don't. I eventually started performing illusions professionally, from high school through college and beyond.

Later, whether writing a play while studying in Germany in college, improving my photography skills in China, or learning to design my own furniture, there was always a common thread. With each new creation, I experienced this combination of joy and wonder. I knew what I was making was more than fun, but I couldn't tell you why.

It was much later in life that I made the connections and realized that this mystery of making had many of the same characteristics as the mystery of faith.

MY REASONS FOR WRITING THIS BOOK

It is that intersection of creativity and faith, that led me to write this book. I've been a follower of Jesus since I was in college. And I realize in hindsight, I've had questions all along about how God works in and through us to do anything, but especially something creative. Over time, my curiosity about faith and making has grown into a passion. It's a quest, really, to explore how my faith affects my creativity—and vice versa—in ways I can apply to create better, and to enjoy a deeper relationship with God. In both the enjoyable moments of inspiration, flow, and joy, and in the hard ones. Those where you feel frustrated or stuck and the way forward seems not just hidden, but as unlikely as a unicorn running up to you and whispering (in that breathy way only unicorns do) the winning ticket number for the next lottery.

This intersection of faith and making lies at the heart of creating adventurously. We'll start in Part I with my journey. I discovered that getting unstuck creatively had everything to do with my identity, calling, faith and, most of all, God's grace. Adventurous creating begins from a place of knowing who you are in Christ (identity). From that firm foundation, we find freedom to explore and work through the four essential elements you need to create, which we cover in Part II. And finally, in Part III, we'll examine the often-surprising, generally paradoxical, and always practical tools that most help you create adventurously.

If you're antsy to understand this concept of creating adventurously, you could jump ahead to whatever chapter seems most appealing for your current needs. But here's a better tip: You already know what it's like. Think of when you felt the greatest joy making something. It likely has traces of that childlike delight you knew as a kid when there was no sense of stuckness, no impostor syndrome, no comparison to others, no feeling of inadequacy or inability, no worrying about the next step because you were so caught up in the bliss of this one. It's where you experienced momentum and felt you were in complete control of the work you were making, even as you were helplessly caught up in its pull. You felt bold, excited, and incredibly grateful just to be doing this work in which you were both lost and found.

That's what it feels like to create adventurously. The goal of this book is to give you a framework or way of thinking, and tools that become the guide rails to help you spend more time in that feeling, that place of both purpose and passion. You won't find prescriptive paint-by-numbers rules here because those rarely show up in the realms of creativity or faith. Instead, you'll find principles, practices, and techniques to make your own way through The Creative Wild. And most of all, as you'll read over and over in the following pages, you have the Spirit of the Living God in, with, and for you at each step. That's a pretty powerful combo for creating.

That's also enough background.

Now, it's time for you to find your pony.

PART I

Spiritual Foundations for Creating Adventurously

In which the hero (you) learns how the real hero (God) fits into this crazy thing we call creativity and how you may be far more of an Adventurous Creative than you realize.

CHAPTER 1
IDENTITY, CALLING, AND GRACE

Where you learn about my journey to getting unstuck, the role of grace in creativity and identity, and how a clearer sense of calling overcomes deeper stuckness.

...the great divide is not between those who are artists and those who are not, but between those who understand that they are creative and those who have become convinced that they are not.

— Erwin Raphael McManus, *The Artisan Soul*

I was stuck.

Or so the two other writers in my critique group told me as I was writing my first book. They said I was operating too much from my head instead of my heart. Both were therapists. Which was fine until they suggested I see a therapist. I pointed out their bias. They demurred. They noted that my stuckness in writing ran deep. And so, after much push back, I visited a therapist.

I went in wanting a quick set of tips on how to get unstuck and write more emotionally. Ever been in counseling? Then you know the direct path ain't gonna happen. They're not there to give you answers, but to help you ask the right questions and find your own answers. *Yeah, yeah, yeah. Just tell me what I need to work on.* That was my main thought. Until my counselor, after getting to know me and my goals a bit, asked a single question:

"What do you most long to do?"

Simple, yes? Easy, no. The question destroyed me.

Within seconds, I couldn't stop the tears. I wasn't even sure why I was crying. But the question in that safe context broke through to something deep inside me. Finally, all I could say was what first came to me.

"Create. I think God made me to be creative."

It wasn't that I hadn't realized before then that I had creative abilities. But I had never allowed myself to embrace "creative" as core to my *identity*, that creating was and is one of the deepest and most significant parts of who I am. I had been stuck in the limiting belief that my creativity mattered to God only if I used it in some direct, practical manner to help others. To accept that creating is good and that being creative is who God made me to be was a bewildering, overwhelming, wondrous, and unexpected revelation. A liberation, really. Hence the tears. Tears of relief, surprise, sadness, and joy all at the same time.

It didn't seem possible. Yet then and ever since, I realize it is true. Not just for me, but for so many of us who yearn to heed that inner call to make something beautiful, something important, or just *something*. And what I discovered there in the therapist's office was that though the words came from my mouth, what so moved me was that the voice was more than mine.

It was the voice of grace.

GRACE AND IDENTITY

Grace, to me, is the most unbelievable thing in the universe. It's God's gift, to those of us who don't deserve it, of unconditional love and forgiveness. It's his promise to always be with us, his acceptance of us just as we are, even as he works to make us into more than we are. It's not just an eternal "get out of jail free" card. It's an ongoing invitation to an intimate relationship with the God of all creation. If you think creativity is a mystery, try wrapping your brain around grace.

I went to the therapist because I thought I was stuck in my writing. I left the therapist realizing just how much I'd been stuck in my deeper sense of who I am, who God is, and how much his grace is a part of all of this. It's a common scenario. We think we're stuck because we're not skilled, experienced, connected, successful, or whatever, enough. But we're unable to progress because we don't look deep enough into where and how we're really stuck.

For me and for many of us, we feel stuck in our jobs, relationships, or a particular project because we don't realize that the deeper issue is spiritual.

As poet Christian Wiman notes:

It is a strange thing how sometimes merely to talk honestly of God, even if it is only to articulate our feelings of separation and confusion, can bring peace to our spirits. You thought you were unhappy because this or that was off in your relationship, this or that was wrong in your job, but the reality is that your sadness stemmed from your aversion to, your stalwart avoidance of, God. The other problems may very well be true, and you will have to address them, but what you feel when releasing yourself to speak of the deepest needs of your spirit is the fact that no other needs could be spoken of outside of that context. You cannot work on the structure of your life if the ground of your being is unsure.[1]

The "ground of my being" was unsure because I had been stuck in a lifelong limiting belief about the role, value, and depth of creativity in my life. When that shifted, so too did my appreciation for God's grace, which, in turn, affected my sense of identity and calling.

One of my favorite explanations of vocation (as calling was once known before "vocation" became more career oriented) comes from the late Frederick Buechner, who defined vocation this way:

It comes from the Latin vocare, to call, and means the work a man is called to by God.

There are all different kinds of voices calling you to all different kinds of work, and the problem is to find out which is the voice of God rather than of Society, say, or the Super-ego, or Self-Interest.

By and large a good rule for finding out is this. The kind of work God usually calls you to is the kind of work (a) that you need most to do and (b) that the world most needs to have done. If you really get a kick out of your work, you've presumably met requirement (a), but if your work is writing TV deodorant commercials, the chances are you've missed requirement (b). On the other hand, if your work is being a doctor in a leper colony, you have probably met requirement (b), but if most of the time you're bored and depressed by it, the chances are you have not only bypassed (a) but probably aren't helping your patients much either.

Neither the hair shirt nor the soft berth will do. The place God calls you to is the place where your deep gladness and the world's deep hunger meet.[2]

I like the simplicity of Buechner's expression, since understanding calling has always been challenging. For example, prior to the Reformation, the prevalent belief was that some callings were "holier" than others. Martin Luther refuted such thinking by noting that the milkmaid serves God just as well in her calling of milking cows as the priest does in his role in the church. That was revolutionary then. Even today, many feel that if you're, say, a missionary, nurse, or doctor, you're doing God's will and serving him and society more than if you're, say, a florist, dancer, or programmer. But according to Luther, each of us can serve and glorify God equally well in whatever role we're in.

Thus, if you've been told that you should focus on more serious work, that your creative efforts are "a nice little side interest," or if you yourself look at more "practical" roles and think, "Now that's *real* ministry" (or a better use of your time), STOP. That is not likely the voice of God. And yet, that's exactly what I bought into for so many years before that culminating moment in the therapist's office with the simple question, "What do you most long to do?"

That moment was pivotal because until then, when I thought about Buechner's phrase, I leaned toward the side of meeting "the world's deep hunger." I liked the notion of "your deep gladness" but honestly, I didn't quite trust it. I figured that if I pursued my own deep gladness, it would lead me away from God. I somehow believed that to be pleasing to God, I had to focus on what I thought was the calling side: the service, the duty, the obedience. I still believe that serving and obeying matter. But what I had missed was that I could do so *through* my deep gladness, not by going around it.

THE GRACE IN CALLING AND VICE VERSA

Over time, I realized how much God's grace weaves its way through his calling. That calling is both purpose *and* relationship, doing *and* being, all bundled together. As a result, it encompasses how I am—and you are—uniquely wired. And if I lean into that—that my deepest desires and God's deepest purposes for me may be the same—all my receptors light up and my relationship with God grows deeper. It's like the line from the movie *Chariots of Fire*: "When I run, I feel God's pleasure." I sense this most when I'm creating. It's not just about what I should do. It's about who I am and how my very relationship with God seems more vibrant when I'm operating in line with the unique way he wired me.

When I grasped this, I no longer saw creating as needing some pragmatic end goal. This drawing doesn't have to make a point. That little moss terrarium doesn't need to convey a message. Instead, I realized that perhaps the whole point of creating may be simply to create. It reminds me of this line from author Anne Lamott: "It's like discovering that while you thought you needed the tea ceremony for the caffeine, what you really needed was the tea ceremony."³ For me, I now realize this: *While I thought I needed to create for an extrinsic purpose, what I really needed was just to create.*

The irony, of course, is that the more I learn to create just for its own sake, the clearer my sense of purpose becomes and the more helpful I am to others. I'll explain more about that wondrous paradox in later chapters. But for now, if you need help, as I did, in grasping the value of creating for its own sake, consider this: Why did God create the world? He had and has perfect fellowship within the Triune Godhead. He didn't *need* us as creatures to relate to, although I have a hunch relationship is still part of the answer, that God creates out of love. I suspect however, that another maybe less obvious answer is that being a Creator, God simply delights in both creating and in what he creates. That maybe, just maybe, so can we. That creating has value. Period.

ADJUSTING PERSPECTIVE

Another part of my limiting belief was that my creative work always needs to help others directly. If not, it means I'm just making things for my own selfish purposes, pursuing self-expression rather than serving people.

The problem with any form of legalism is that it is hard to argue with. How can helping others, as in "love your neighbor as yourself," be anything but our highest aim after "love the Lord with all our heart, soul, mind, and strength" (Mark 12:30-31)? The answer, or at least part of it, is that there are an infinite number of ways to do this. Unfortunately, as we'll see in the chapter on Environment, in many Christian circles we've narrowly defined what it means to love others, share Jesus with them, care for those in need, pursue justice, minister to our neighbors, etc. But as creatives, part of our role can be prophetic in revealing alternative approaches.

What's helped me shift my understanding is appreciating anew just how mysterious creativity, like grace, is. We neither understand it completely nor comprehend the impact that our actions can have on others or—this is key—on ourselves. Creating just for yourself may seem selfish—until you become the "ten-year overnight sensation." When I expand my thinking—and my limited view of God, his grace, and his timing—I realize this: We don't know how God will prepare, use, or shape us as a result of our creative efforts, even those done in private just for us.

When I was in grad school, I attended a meeting of the campus's Christian fellowship. One evening, a speaker talked about her work in a refugee camp in Thailand. After the presentation, I spoke privately with the woman. She asked if I might be interested in coming to work there. I laughed and told her, "Tomorrow at 7:00 a.m., I get on an airplane to Chicago to interview with an advertising agency. You tell me what advertising skills have to do with those needed in a refugee camp."

The speaker replied, "You may not use your advertising skills in a refugee camp directly, but that's not the point. God uses all your diverse abilities and experiences, no matter the area, to shape your character and who you are. And it is your character that he can use. Anywhere."

What you do today—even work no one yet sees—may have a profound effect later in meeting the world's deep hunger. You just don't know right now. You can't. And best of all, you don't have to. God does. When you treat your creative work as an act of faith and trust God to use it in the ways he wants, you're freed to create for its own sake and enjoy God more in the process. Your only job is to follow your calling, do the work, give God the glory, and leave the results to him.

Through all you do, even efforts that feel about as creative as a handshake, you begin to recognize how deeply entwined grace and relationship are with calling and purpose. This is the route to discovering that creating—your own deep gladness—has value in itself.

When I connected the dots between stuckness, identity, calling, and grace, so much started falling into place, particularly around my sense of who I am creatively and my creative work. But I also discovered something more. If I want to enjoy my work more now and increase the odds of staying unstuck, a powerful—and surprising—approach is to be more intentional in inviting God into that creative work. And to recognize not just the challenges of being stuck, but the benefits. Let's explore both in the next chapter.

QUESTIONS AND EXPLORATIONS
- Do you see yourself as a creative person? Do others see you as that? How about as an artist? What do you feel when you say out loud (even if no one else is around), "I am an adventurous creative"?
- For you, what does the "world's deep hunger and your deep gladness" look like? Where do the two meet?
- In what ways do you feel stuck? Write these down as we'll come back to them later. In any of those, do you think there may be deeper issues that are leading to the symptoms you're facing? What might those be?

CHAPTER 2
STUCKNESS, ABIDING, AND CREATING AS AN ACT OF GRACE

Where you learn what the attributes are of an Adventurous Creative, how Jesus is both creative and adventurous, and how stuckness can be core to creating adventurously.

...I can say confidently that the number one obstacle the modern person faces when it comes to prayer is an inability to receive the love of God...We buy that intellectually, but at a deeper level, somewhere in our emotions, in our bones, we don't trust it...The second we forget (that God loves us), the second it's diluted into a trope or held in the intellect while a story of our sufficiency or control or performance lives in our bones, our lives unravel, and so does our faith.
— Tyler Staton, *Praying Like Monks, Living Like Fools*

Your journey through The Creative Wild will always contain moments of being stuck and moments of grace. Believe it or not, the two go together. That's one of the most surprising and hopeful paradoxes of The Creative Wild. What you may now consider to be negative pauses or setbacks may, instead, be opportunities for grace—small, unexpected gifts that become essential elements in your ability to create adventurously.

HOW WE GET STUCK BEING STUCK

Much of how you handle or embrace getting stuck comes down to how you view the very idea of being stuck. If you're like me, you've got more ways to get stuck than an airport full of holiday travelers in a blizzard. But what I've found in talking with creative people is that their very thinking about stuckness can contribute to the problem. We tend to either underestimate or overinflate its impact on us.

On the underestimating side, some people don't even know they are stuck creatively. They may, like me, not realize how much certain limiting beliefs have throttled their creative identity or that their stuckness goes deeper than the emotional or psychological into the spiritual. Or if they do embrace their creativity, they may go about the same routines, making similar work without realizing they are no longer creating. They are only producing. They are stuck in their habits, ways, and mindsets without being conscious of it.

On the overinflating side, there's a bit of a lemming in each of us. When you hear so much from those around you about writer's block or being stuck in the wrong job or not knowing what to do with your life, it's easy to believe you too are stuck. You may, however, just be dealing with the usual difficulties of life or creating. What I hope to do in this book is not only give you tools for getting unstuck (or better, not getting stuck to begin with) but also a perspective that shifts how you think about the subject.

By the time you're done here, you will discover that much of what may seem like a negative about getting stuck can be used in your favor. For example, we'll explore how frustration isn't the exception in creating, but the norm. Or how, by overcoming the compartmentalization of your creativity and faith, you can enhance both. Or how what may feel like getting stuck is actually the natural cadence of creating, the dynamic of tension and release that lies at the heart of making. In short, much of what we think of as friction may, in fact, be traction. What we believe to be a stall may be a helpful period of waiting. And what we consider a roadblock may be a detour, in God's hands, to a better destination.

Just look at great literature or films if you want another example of how stuckness is core to our greatest accomplishments. In virtually every memorable story, the hero is stuck. Moses is stuck tending sheep for forty years. Odysseus is stuck on his voyage and can't get home. Elizabeth Bennet is stuck in her own pride and prejudice. Luke Skywalker is stuck on his uncle's farm. Without an obstacle to overcome, there is no hero's journey. Creativity involves problem solving. And almost all forms of stuckness are just problems awaiting our creative solutions. Thus, part of creating adventurously is seeing getting stuck more as an aid than an adversary.

Another part is recognizing just how much grace runs through all of what it means to create adventurously, including those points of stuckness. Getting stuck redirects our attention and energy and, in that process, we are often rerouted to a new—a better—direction or journey's end. God uses our stuckness (often in surprising ways) to refine both us and our work. For example, and maybe you can relate, often when I get stuck, I doubt myself. My sense of worth and value can plummet, and I can start to lose all grounding in my identity as a beloved child of God. But when I see stuckness as a form of grace—the prospect of a wondrous pony hidden amid the dross—something remarkable occurs. I recognize this pause isn't intended to hinder me, but to get my attention and alert me to the possibility of God doing something amazing through, for, and with me.

Such an awareness provides a spiritual safety net that also helps me to be bolder in taking creative risks. I'm more confident when I grasp, as Philip Yancey puts it, that through grace, there is nothing we can do to make God love us more and nothing we can do to make God love us less. That knowledge comforts me in difficult times, grounds me in the giddy moments of creative success, and supports me when nothing makes sense. Risk of any kind is easier to embrace when you know you are beloved, delighted in, and not alone.

CREATING AS AN ACT OF GRACE

What has also helped me has been a kind of reframing—from seeing grace as a theological concept I believe in, to seeing it as an undeserved blessing I inhabit, particularly when making. When I see it this way, all aspects of creating are a gift, one I receive, embrace, and share. I hold my own skills, talents, and opportunities loosely because I know they are gifts, not obligations or things I deserve or have earned. I then abide with God to use these in new ways. Finally, I give the results of my creative efforts—at least the ones I don't do just for me—to others. It's my own small way of meeting the world's deep hunger. Yes, I may charge for them if those efforts are part of my business. But this mindset has little to do with compensation. Instead, it's about my attitude and a grace-full spirit.

That attitude means that all the things I'm prone to fret about—excellence, purpose, relevance, adequacy, acceptance, and even identity—*feel* different when I see making in the context of grace. Creating shifts from the pressure to make something original or profound, to honoring the creative drive, glorifying God, and acknowledging that my unique ability is a gift from him. I no longer have to prove to myself or anyone else that I can do this. Instead, it's more a call and response of abiding and experiencing the joy of using the gifts God has given me. It is my deep gladness in action.

I still need to care about my audiences (for I have more than one) and what they want and need. But seeing my work as a gift to them diminishes the concerns of "will they like this?" or worse, "will they like me?" I shift who's in the driver's role by offering my work first, as unto the Lord, and second, to my audiences as a gift. Even for paying clients, viewing a project as a generous act changes the equation. I'm less apt to take rejection personally because my goal isn't for them to like me or even the work, but simply to bless them.

This blessing applies to us as well. Grace is knowing at the level of our core identity that we are loved and worthy, and that God is ever-present with us no matter how stuck we feel or how far we may wander or fall short. It's the sureness that your identity does not change even when a project stalls, no one comes to your opening, or a client criticizes your work. Grace helps you keep creating because it releases you from the need to be perfect in order to be lovable and worthy.

ABIDING AND CREATING

I'm most aware of this sense of grace when I seek to intentionally abide with Jesus in the process of creating. God never goes away, but sometimes I do. I forget my first love. I wander and cease to seek him with any of my heart, much less all of it (Jeremiah 29:13). In desperation, I will invite God into my sorrow and struggles, but later, neglect to invite him into my joy. But when I remember my soul's longing for his presence and incorporate that into the delight of creating, both increase. I find it easier to "keep in step with the Spirit" (Galatians 5:25) when I'm making, and more rewarding to create when I'm abiding with God. Most of all, I get stuck a lot less often. At the risk of getting into too deep of theological language, it's like a double-whammy of bliss, a win-win on a cosmic level, my very, very happy place. And it all starts with abiding.

Abiding is one of those King James version words that is so old, it can seem fresh today. To abide means to spend time with someone, to, in the words of John 15:4, "remain in him." Abiding is relational. I'm not sure there's a wrong way to do this if your desire is to be with Jesus. It's an intentional decision to remember that the Holy Spirit is with you and empowers you as you create. For me, it means in part, making the process more conversational. I will at times pause my work and simply praise God or say, "What's next?" "Thank you for that idea or this result," "This is so cool!" "Let's do this," or "Is this the right direction?" Then I listen to see if an idea presents itself or I receive guidance. If not, I press on and stay attuned to however God may want to show up. It's usually more about resting in his presence or anticipating how he might surprise me than demanding his attention or action.

The real value anyway isn't in having projects turn out better. Sounds strange, doesn't it? After all, don't we invite God in to improve our creative outcomes? Hmmm. I'm not sure it works that way. I think my creative work is better now than it used to be, but that could be because my skills have improved over time. But I can say that the *process* of making is substantively better. In other words, you may not see much change in the fruits of your labor. But you will likely see in your life an increase in the Fruits of the Spirit such as love, joy, peace, patience, etc. (Galatians 5:22-23). Creating is fraught with insecurity and worry. And yet I have noticed that when I abide, those have far less a hold on me.

IN SUMMARY

Through all of this, in good moments and ones that make a bad hair day seem downright cheerful, we abide. Creativity, as we shall see, has distinct periods of frustration where you can feel stuck. You can't get around that. But as novelist Haruki Murakami noted about long-distance running, "Pain is inevitable. Suffering is optional." Creating is often painful, but you don't have to suffer, as the myth of the tortured artist would suggest.

When you create as an act of grace, stuckness loses its grip on you, especially when you see elements of grace in moments that otherwise might seem like setbacks. You can maintain a sense of hope and joy even when things are hard. You can magnify that joy by inviting God into the creative process and viewing all your creative efforts through the lens of grace. In so doing, the work no longer becomes the most important thing. The One you do it for and with is. And that doesn't just change your work. It changes your life.

QUESTIONS AND EXPLORATIONS

- What might this idea of "creating as an act of grace" look like in your life? How might the notion of creating as a gift from God free you to create more adventurously in ways that bless others?
- Is there a word or phrase other than "abiding" that works better for you in terms of remaining in him or being present to God in all you do? What baby steps could you take to either abide with God while you create or do so more consistently?
- Have you ever considered being stuck as a blessing? For each of the examples you wrote down at the end of the last chapter, what might be ways you could see them in a positive light?

CHAPTER 3
CREATING ADVENTUROUSLY

Where you discover what the attributes are of an Adventurous Creative, how Jesus is both creative and adventurous, and how stuckness can be core to creating adventurously.

For their short while on earth, most people long to have the fullest life they can. No-one wants to remain a prisoner in an unlived life. This was the intention of Jesus: 'I have come that you may have life and have it to the full.' Of the many callings in the world, the invitation to the adventure of an awakened and full life is the most exhilarating. This is the dream of every heart. Yet most of us are lost or caught in forms of life that exile us from the life we dream of. Most people long to step onto the path of creative change that would awaken their lives to beauty and passion, deepen their contentment and allow their lives to make a difference.

— John O'Donohue, *Beauty*

When I was writing my previous book, *Hidden Travel*, I asked my friend Andy how he'd summarize the theme of that book. He responded, "That's easy: 'You were made for adventure.'" Good answer.

One definition of adventure is this:

"An adventure is an exciting experience or undertaking that is typically bold, sometimes risky."[4]

Many people associate adventure with thrill-seeking. But adventure is relative. For one person, adventure might mean navigating Class V rapids in a kayak. For another, it might mean trying something spicier than a tomato for the first time (and yes, I discovered on a trip to Minnesota once that some people consider tomatoes to be spicy). We all sense that without stretching in our lives, we won't grow. Growth requires risk because risk means you're venturing into the unknown. Which is what artists and creatives do every time they make something new.

Psychotherapist Esther Perel has studied relationships for decades. She has found that all marriages balance an ongoing tension between the need for safety and freedom. Humans want both security and adventure. But we get mixed up about when, how, and to what degree we desire each. We are no different with creating.

You can be a creative adventurer, someone who incorporates their creative interests into their trips and activities. Or an adventurous creative, someone who approaches making as *"an exciting experience or undertaking that is typically bold, sometimes risky."* Or, perhaps, a bit of both. Either way, creating adventurously doesn't imply you'll be bungee jumping with a can of spray paint in hand or doing exhibitionistic performance art (though it could). Instead, creating adventurously could encompass quiet adventures, the simple pleasures of making, and pursuing small moments of challenge and wonder.

TAKING WISE RISKS

Creating adventurously is more about taking wise risks that result in a state of flow versus undertaking a risk for the adrenaline rush of overstimulation for its own sake. Thrill seekers pursue risk for the resulting emotion. Creatives pursue risks to elevate their work for a specific purpose or outcome. Much of this relates to temperament and personality. You're likely to find as many thrill-seeking artists as there are flow-seeking ones. And sometimes, it is hard to tell the difference. Like everything in this book, it comes down to finding what works for you. It's not about defining your level of risk acceptance. It's more about being curious and passionate enough about an idea that you shift your focus from fear of the risk to creative desire. Connection to passion helps us move past fear and take the risk.

When there's a photograph I feel I must take, I'll climb down a mist-slick cliff face (within reason) to get the shot. At any other time, I'd be too wary to even lean over the edge. I'll perform in front of vast crowds if it is *my* presentation or show. But ask me to volunteer before a handful of people and I'll timidly decline. It's not an ego or introvert/extrovert issue, so much as caring enough about the creative element to not notice that I'm way out of my comfort zone.

WHAT IT MEANS TO BE AN ADVENTUROUS CREATIVE

Willingness to take wise risks when it seems appropriate is just one of the many elements of creating adventurously. We'll unpack each of these in the coming chapters, but for now, just be aware that an adventurous creative:

- Adheres to a both/and approach while abiding with Jesus and seeing creating as an act of grace (Chapter 2).
- Pursues mastery not as a goal they reach but as a continuum they're on (Chapter 4).
- Leverages place, space, and other environmental factors for their best work (Chapters 5 and 13).
- Maintains a state of readiness and an awareness of their own assets, agency, and the rhythms that work best for them (Chapters 7 and 8).
- Practices re-creation to discover more and improve faster (Chapters 9 and 10).
- Keeps moving, makes stuckness work for them, and sustains momentum (Chapter 11).
- Is adept at reframing and using their unique voice (Chapter 12).
- Works for and with others and pursues something bigger than themselves (Chapter 14).

- Knows when and how to use indirection and incompletion (Chapters 15 and 16).
- Seeks rightness and resonance in, through, and for their creative work (Chapter 17).

How each of these manifests in your life and creative work will probably look different than others—and even you—expect. That's in part because of the mystery inherent in making and how God hides future steps from us so we stay in close fellowship with him as we create. But one thing that all adventurous creatives share is this sense of action and participation, engaging in your creative life rather than being a spectator. Entering that hot kitchen rather than watching it on the Food Network. Jumping in when you don't feel ready, realizing that's the only way you will. And building in you a greater awareness of grace along with a heightened spirit of ingenuity and the adventurous capacity to figure out what to do when you're unsure.

FOLLOWING GOD'S LEAD IN CREATING ADVENTUROUSLY

All of this would be aspirational, inspirational rah-rah talk if it weren't for your Guide. We have God's grace and the Holy Spirit empowering us to do this. And we have Jesus as a model of someone who was both creative and adventurous. Even if you overlook the minor detail of Jesus as the Word of God who created the entire world, his creativity shows up throughout the Gospels. He told stories, outsmarted his critics, leveraged miracles to make points, and developed his disciples—all creative endeavors. He also engaged his whole body, not just in an Incarnational sense, but in a creative one. Most of his responses involved touch and physicality—head, heart, and hands—not just intellectual replies. And let's not forget that he was a carpenter. (As a woodworker myself, I'm not saying that's the reason I became a Christian. But it didn't hurt.)

In terms of being adventurous, Jesus was always on the move, going into risky situations, and tackling new challenges. He never shied away from conflict. He always spoke not just what was true, but what most needed to be said, often in surprising and improvisational ways. He led a very *daring*—a word that applies to both creating and adventure—life.

It's funny though. Unless prompted to do so (as I'm doing here), we don't normally consider Jesus in this light. But that's the point. You may not think of yourself in these daring ways either, and yet, here you are. It's no accident or coincidence you're reading this.

The point of this book isn't to make you into something you're not. It's to help you become *more* of who you already are, whether you realize or accept it yet. And when you embrace that this is who you were born to be, something inside you clicks. You suspect that, like Aslan in Narnia, the way forward isn't safe. But it is good, because you move through all of this with and for Jesus. He's what makes creating adventurously doable when things get hard. That's in part because in the hard places is where we most find life. But it is also where we most find him, always present, always desiring our best. He's the one who motivates us to continue and who supports us when we don't know how.

With Jesus, learning to create adventurously means that you become free of the fear of doing things wrong or doing the wrong things. Instead, you embrace the joy of discovery. You see every project as an opportunity to explore and learn, rather than a potential masterpiece you might mess up. You take a lifelong view of creativity as part of your identity, a muscle you grow over time, one that applies to all areas of your life.

THE WAY FORWARD

Hopefully, I've given you a good sense of what it means to create adventurously. But if you want the simplest way of summing it up, here's a piece of advice given to me a few years ago. It didn't sound like much more than a variation on a familiar athletic company's tagline at first. But over the years, I've come to appreciate the wisdom.

I was in the Cappadocia region of Turkey, and through a set of connections and so-called coincidences, I met with one of the country's top photographers. He invited me to his home—which was carved out of a cliff face overlooking a gorgeous valley lined with other cave-like homes distinctive to this region. His home contained works of art of all kinds, down to the handmade cabinets, utensils, and furniture in the kitchen where he served me tea. As I marveled at it all, I asked him, "So all of this, this beauty that you inhabit, is it art or craft?" He smiled, paused, then responded, "Art or craft? It doesn't matter. Only one thing does and that is this: Just make something!"

Since that day, whenever I lose enthusiasm, feel stuck, wonder about my purpose, or question if what I'm doing creatively is pleasing to God or the best use of my time (or any of a hundred other questions that have an edge of "should" over grace) I recall his response. And then I heed his advice. I make.

It is in the making where I find that sense of congruence between desire, purpose, and relationship. And in creating *adventurously,* I get all that along with a spirit of hopeful possibility and connection. I embrace this moment even as I look forward to others. In abiding with God as I make, I feel like the little child who is overjoyed simply to be playing with their father. Who delights in his presence, but also in the fun they have doing something together. And most of all, who cries out in ebullient anticipation, "Surprise me, Daddy!" knowing, without doubt, that he will.

No matter your age, you have a lifetime before you of creative possibility, an adventure God is inviting you to undertake. It's a way to know him and glorify him even as you experience greater joy and purpose. It means saying yes to new opportunities, knowing that you are kept close to the One who goes with you, even in those times where he may feel distant or you feel stuck. This is an adventure, after all. Not everything will go as planned. But that's not why we undertake adventures. We do so because we were made for them. And if you ever get stuck or become lost in believing this, if your identity feels hidden or faded, or if your sense of purpose becomes confused, don't worry. I've got a solution for you.

Just make something.

QUESTIONS AND EXPLORATIONS

- Do you think of yourself as adventurous? In what ways? Is it a characteristic you'd like to see more of in your life? How about in your creative work?
- The slogan of a church I once visited was this: "A safe place to live dangerously." Where, in your life, do you have such places? Physically? Emotionally? Spiritually? Relationally?
- Does the imperative to "just make something" encourage you? Or does it somewhat frustrate you because you don't know what to make? If the latter, don't worry. You'll have a better sense of that as we go. But just for fun, without overthinking, if you could make just one thing right now, irrespective of cost, time, medium, or market viability, what would it be? What does that tell you?

PART II

Essentials for Creating Adventurously

In which the hero (you), comes to understand that you only need four essentials to create—Motivation, Mastery, Mindset, and a supportive Environment—and then one of three optional approaches—a roadmap, rules, or intuition—to navigate The Creative Wild.

CHAPTER 4
MINDSET, MASTERY, AND MOTIVATION

Where you learn why knowing creative techniques (not just subject-matter expertise) is key to creating well, why mastery is a continuum, and ways to reignite motivation.

Whether you think you can or think you can't—you're right.
— **Henry Ford**

May the favor of the Lord our God rest on us; establish the work of our hands for us—yes, establish the work of our hands.
— **Psalm 90:17**

When confronted with a challenge, the committed heart will search for a solution. The undecided heart searches for an escape.
— **Andy Andrews**

Although The Creative Wild is a mysterious place, we do know four elements that are essential to making your way through it and doing excellent creative work:

- Mindset
- Mastery
- Motivation
- Environment (sorry, I couldn't figure out a good "M" word for this other than maybe "Milieu" and that sounds too swamp-like or fancy).

These elements are rather intuitive. You need the right attitude, approach, and mental tools (Mindset). You need skills in your chosen medium or field (Mastery). You must want to do the work (Motivation). And finally, you need both people and a place that nurtures your creative efforts (Environment).

In his book, *The Myths of Creativity,* David Burkus notes how the research of Teresa Amabile, a Harvard Business School professor, supports the importance of these four essentials.[5] In that research, she points out an important nuance: You need skills in your domain (mastery of your subject or medium) PLUS specific know-how in the creative process itself (which I'm grouping under mindset), in addition to motivation and a supportive environment to succeed. This is where so many otherwise creative people never achieve their potential. They focus only on mastering skills related to their work, but not on understanding the creative process and the critical role of mindset. The good news is that this book will give you that understanding of the creative process and corresponding creative mindset tools to augment your subject-matter expertise.

We're going to explore the "3Ms" here in this chapter, then look at environment in the next. After these four essentials, we'll look at some optional approaches that differ for each person as they navigate The Creative Wild. For now, however, let's start in this chapter with mindset since it can aid or undermine all the others.

MINDSET

Mindset matters because you can have all the desire (motivation) in the world and an amazing set of skills (mastery). But if your attitude is off or your underlying beliefs undermine your goals, your chances of creating adventurously—or at all—take on the glide path of a dropped piano.

The American Heritage Dictionary defines mindset as: "A way of thinking; an attitude or opinion, especially a habitual one." But that definition is so wide, you could, well, drop a baby grand through it. Mindset can cover so many areas, including our predispositions, such as in Carol Dweck's work on fixed mindsets (believing you are limited to the way you are) and growth mindsets (believing you can change). Thus, for our purposes here, I'll restrict "mindset" to being mostly about knowhow of the creative process (covered in Chapter 6 and throughout Part III), attitude (which we explore in depth in Chapter 12, Perspective), and your underlying core beliefs. I shared two of my limiting core beliefs about creativity earlier, but here are some others I've held, along with my current perspectives. I offer them mostly to show that while some core beliefs run so deep you may need counseling to address them, most dealing with creativity are ones you can overcome with time, prayer, and new habits. See if any of these sound familiar:

- Then: I'm just not talented enough in _____ (drawing, sculpting, singing, writing, cooking, etc.) therefore I can never be creative in those areas.
  — Now: I don't have to be talented. I just need to practice and enjoy the process of making.
- Then: I'm not as good as so-and-so so why bother trying.
  — Now: Bring it on and ignore comparisons. Trying new things stretches me and I can enjoy the challenge even if I'm no good at it.
- Then: If I can't immediately be at least decent at this new thing, then I never will be.
  — Now: If I practice, I can get better at almost anything. Also, perfectionism isn't a commitment to excellence. It's a fear of not being good enough. So I hold on to this verse, appreciating the irony of the adjective used: "*Perfect* love casts out fear" (1 John 4:18).
- Then: I don't have the time to learn a new skill.
  — Now: I don't have time not to. If I stop learning, some part of me dies or shrivels up like Voldemort in the final Harry Potter movie.

- Then: There are already too many people doing this thing. Why bother being just one more?
  — Now: So? I can still find my own little niche using my unique voice. Plus, there's far more to gain from cooperation than competition.
- Then: God values creativity if it leads people to Jesus and if not, it's of secondary importance.
  — Now: We've already seen part of the answer in the early chapters of this book. Creativity matters in itself and we don't know the end of the story, so what we do alone today could change the world tomorrow.
- Then: Creative people dress funny.
  — Now: Well, I still believe this in some circles. But most of the creative people I know dress like anyone else. And for those with the crazy wardrobes or bling? Now I appreciate the look. Well, most of the time.

MASTERY

Think of mastery less as an end state and more as a progression similar to your health. You can maintain it, improve it, or let it slip. With mastery, it's more than the expansion of your skills in a particular creative area. It's an accumulation of experience that not only aids in technique, but also in wisdom.

When you master one area or medium, learning others, even in unrelated fields, comes easier. For example, I can apply the design skills of composition and cropping I learn from photography to drawing or painting (and vice versa) and even evaluating visual identity work in branding. In all areas, I now have a "better eye" and more trustworthy instincts. This and other forms of mastery are a kind of "knack" or embodied know-how that you develop—an intuitive (as opposed to conscious) grasp of the creative process that, like prayer, you only develop through doing.

You could consider this ability to excel in an area as talent, but talent too lies on a continuum and is only the starting point for mastery. Sure, you need a baseline level of skills: You likely won't be in the NBA if you're five foot two inches. But if you have enough of the basic skills, it is desire, the right mindset, and then dedicated practice (the mastery piece) that will get you to the next level. And the next.

As author Ann Patchett puts it:

Art stands on the shoulders of craft, which means that to get to the art you must master the craft. If you want to write, practice writing. Practice it for hours a day, not to come up with a story you can publish, but because you long to learn how to write well, because there is something that you alone can say. Write the story, learn from it, put it away, write another story. Think of a sink pipe filled with sticky sediment. The only way to get clean water is to force a small ocean through the tap. Most of us are full up with bad stories, boring stories, self-indulgent stories, searing works of unendurable melodrama. We must get all of them out of our system in order to find the good stories that may or may not exist in the freshwater underneath.[6]

LEVELS OF MASTERY

The continuum of mastery in any field builds over time through a series of steps. The Medieval guild system understood this. Their three levels of Mastery align roughly with what we all go through in our own creative journeys:

- **Apprentice:** In this phase you start with, then move out of the initial excitement of learning something new and push through the experiences of boredom, frustration, anxiety, and confusion into a more continuous form of learning, preferably under the tutelage of a mentor or set of mentors. You realize your strengths and rely on them.

- **Journeyman:** Here, you persevere, gain fluency and muscle memory, master essential skills and techniques which enable you to take on more complex work. You then move from student to practitioner, developing your own rhythms and routines, as well as your unique voice and style.
- **Master:** If you continue, you reach a higher level of Mastery where you can trust your instincts, synthesize diverse ideas and inputs, pursue truly innovative ideas, and learn when and how to break the rules. You also learn how to work better with others since mastery is individual in acquisition, but a team sport when it comes to innovation and creativity.[7]

If you're looking at this and thinking, "I've got a long way to go," don't worry. Mastery grows at different rates over time for different creative areas. I'm at the master level in my branding work but wouldn't be allowed near the back door of the video-making guild. And here's the big secret. You only have to master ENOUGH of your medium to get you to the next step. And when you're starting out, the bar is pretty low.

Want to become a painter? Learn how to draw. That starts with being able to hold a pen or pencil and draw a line. Not even a straight one. Can you do that? If so, you're in. Want to be a singer? Can you sing a tune roughly on key? You're in. That's enough to get you on your way for now. You get the point. You only have to be good ENOUGH to start the next step.

FOCUS ON PRACTICING, NOT COMPARING

To get to that next step, practice. Not on what is easy to do, but what is hard. Practice daily, if possible, in the areas you most want to master. Even if it is only for 15 minutes each day. Also, focus on *your* work and *your* journey, not on that of a pro who's been doing it for twenty years. I've found this graph from Mihaly Csikszentmihalyi's book *Flow* to be a helpful guide in terms of Mastery and where to concentrate your practice efforts.

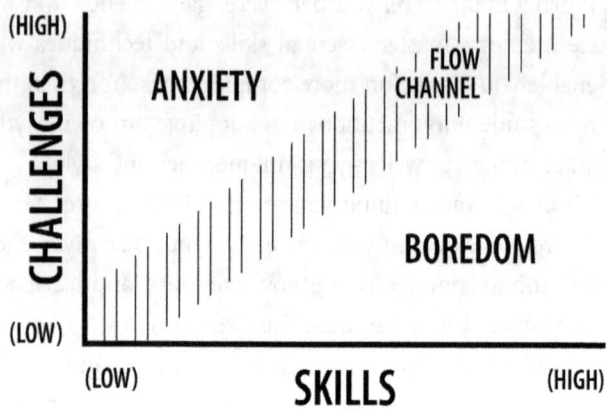

It shows that if your skill level is low and the challenges you face are high, you'll feel anxiety. If you have well-developed skills, but the challenge is low, you'll be bored. The optimal spot, where you most experience flow, is when your challenges match your skill level. Which is why looking at the work of more advanced practitioners in your field can either inspire you or lead you into a place of anxiety if you view their work as something you should be able to do now. You can't—not yet. Which shouldn't overwhelm you but encourage you—increase your motivation—to practice more. Not necessarily to be like them, but because you enjoy it.

MOTIVATION

Motivation for the creative is the deep desire to make something new, beautiful, or valuable. It's like the old line about how many psychiatrists does it take to change a light bulb. One. But the light bulb has to want to change. And so it is with creating. You've got to want to do it. Without that passion to create, all the talent, skill, and mindset tricks won't matter. Creating is hard. But what keeps you in the game is this deep longing and the sense that you *have to* do it.

Your motivation stems from your calling and that intersection of passion, purpose, grace, and relationship. In fact, your relationship with Jesus can be core to what motivates you. When I tap into that deeper longing and belief that it comes from God, I can be drawn to make something even when I don't feel like getting off the couch. It's why professional creatives don't rely on inspiration or other situational factors to create. Their motivation compels them to show up in a workmanlike manner every day, knowing that inspiration will find them.

Motivation gets a lift from inspiration, however, particularly with new areas or media. We've likely all had moments when we saw the work in a medium new to us and we can't believe we've never tried that before. In fact, finding the right medium can be key to your overall creative motivation. Sir Ken Robinson, one of the world's leading experts on creativity in education, found that "Discovering the right medium is often a tidal moment in the creative life of the individual." He adds, "There are many examples of people whose creativity is fired by particular media: not water colors, but pastels, not mathematics in general, but algebra in particular."[8] Vincent Van Gogh's art never took off until he experimented with oil paints. Most professional musicians never reach their highest levels unless they (instead of their parents) select their instrument.

Medium may be what ignites desire, but intrinsic motivation—your internal drive, passion, or sense of purpose—sustains it. Extrinsic rewards such as money and fame can, in some situations, provide motivation. But as Steven Johnson notes in *The Innovator's Cookbook*:

> There is abundant evidence of strong intrinsic motivation in the stories of widely recognized creative people…Albert Einstein talked about intrinsic motivation as 'the enjoyment of seeing and searching.' The novelist John Irving, in discussing the very long hours he put into his writing,

said, 'The unspoken factor is love. The reason I can work so hard at my writing is that it's not work for me.' And Michael Jordan, perhaps the most creative basketball player ever, had a 'love of the game' clause inserted into his contract; he insisted that he be free to play pickup basketball games anytime he wished.[9]

How about you? What motivates you to make or keep making? If you need some assistance with that, I have a list of what motivates me (and another list of what doesn't), along with multiple exercises you can try if you need to identify what motivates you. You can find them at www.ExploreYourWorlds.com/Motivation. In general, when my motivation to make lags or I feel stuck, I may return to that list to remind me. But I also remember the following key points.

First, I recall just how powerful motivation itself is. As Ruth Haley Barton notes:

> *The depth of desire has a great deal to do with the outcome of our life. Often, those who accomplish what they set out to do in life are not those who are the most talented or gifted or who have had the best opportunities. Often, they are the ones who are most deeply in touch with how badly they want whatever they want; they are the ones who consistently refuse to be deterred by the things that many of us allow to become excuses.*[10]

Second, I get to a point where I can't ignore the longing. Amanda Palmer, in her book, *The Art of Asking*, tells the story of a man whose car breaks down near a farm. He's out of cell phone range, so he asks to use the farmer's phone. While waiting on the farmer's porch for the tow truck, the man notices the farmer's dog lying nearby, whimpering. The man asks why the dog is whimpering in pain. "It's because he's lying on a nail," the farmer replies. "But why then doesn't he get up and move?" asks the man. "Don't hurt 'nough yet," says the farmer.

Often for creative types, reconnecting to our passions is a combination of desire and pain. The pain comes from ignoring or putting off the longing until not doing what you most desire becomes unbearable and it hurts enough to move.

Third, when you have the drive, but not the direction, one of the most helpful rules of thumb is one we looked at earlier: Pursue what interests you most right now. Not in general, but at this moment. What am I most curious about now? What do I most want to try? What question won't go away?

If you don't know, make a list of what inspires you: movies, nature, cultural or family traditions, memories, books, going to a museum, visiting a place that sparks your imagination, particular websites, podcasts, music, certain friends, childhood activities, old journals, found objects, artworks, food, drink, travel, doodling, wandering, exercise, observing small things up close or big things from a distance, overhearing strangers' conversations, going some place that scares you (just a little), making something with your hands, taking a different route somewhere, praying, dancing, singing, playing, etc. You can also give yourself a challenge and make this a game or invite others to help or play. Keeping a list of what inspires or interests you sounds simple, but it is a powerful way to home in on what God may be calling you to pursue, as well as to remember why you love that pursuit.

When all else fails, remember the earlier advice: Just make something. Or keep making something. Motivation grows with mastery. The more you make, the more you'll want to make, and vice versa. And doing so will help your mindset and improve your mastery. All three work together to help you get and sustain momentum in The Creative Wild. As does the fourth of the four essentials, a supportive environment. Let's turn to that next.

QUESTIONS AND EXPLORATIONS

- Make a list of your top five limiting beliefs regarding creativity. Then record a corresponding alternative belief, one you'd like to hold even if you currently don't. What could you do to make those alternatives a reality?
- Sir Ken Robinson tells the story of a concert pianist who, in her 40s, realized that while excellent at playing the piano, she didn't enjoy it. She stuck with it only because she excelled at it. She later became a literary editor and loved that job.[11] Is there an area you're good at but don't love? Do you feel you've found your right medium? Is there a different one you'd love to try?
- "As the writer Joshua Foer put it, 'When most musicians sit down to practice, they play the parts of pieces that they're good at. Of course they do; it's fun to succeed. But expert musicians tend to focus on the parts that are hard, the parts they haven't yet mastered.'"[12] How do you practice? How might you do so differently now?

CHAPTER 5
ENVIRONMENT

Where you learn why environment isn't positive or even neutral, why Evangelicals make bad films, why creating propaganda rarely works, and why you have an incredible opportunity because you sit between two cultures.

Change is good. You go first.
— a line written on the side of a Dilbert pen

As much as I might like it to be otherwise, *where* we are almost always affects *who* we are. Our environment—the physical setting, the surrounding people, the temperature or ambience, even our mood at the time or blood sugar levels—will affect us in ways that are as surprising as they are predictable. Especially when creating, affecting us in ways both challenging and good.

We'll explore the more obvious aspects of environment such as your studio, business, performance space, or other place of making in Chapter 13. But in this chapter, let's look at the less intuitive but equally important elements that affect your creativity in ways you likely don't expect.

WHY ENVIRONMENT MATTERS

In his book *Triggers,* Marshall Goldsmith points out how your environment is less like a friendly background setting and more like a minefield. Influences of all kinds—people, sounds, scents, light, hunger, health, the performance of your favorite team in last night's game—can snare you, trigger you, and wreck not just your day, but your overall ability to create. And while we're aware—all too aware—of the screaming child one table over from us at the café where we normally write, other aspects of the environment can affect us without registering consciously. This especially applies to macro environmental influences such as culture.

In the research of Harvard professor Teresa Amabile that I cited earlier, environment referred to factors in a corporate setting such as management, other staff, and how supportive the general office culture is toward creativity. In the Church, it includes attitudes toward innovation and creative people, but goes as far as our theological underpinnings regarding grace, beauty, novelty, and even change. Creatives who follow Jesus live in the borderlands between secular and Christian cultures. They realize how challenging that space can be. But as we're about to see, it also gives us a remarkable opportunity to use our creative efforts in ways that can resonate and connect with both worlds.

UNDERLYING PERCEPTIONS ABOUT CREATIVITY

Behind all of this is the sad reality that people say they value creativity, but when you show up with an innovative idea, they ignore, reject, or even attack it. In the abstract, creativity is a positive thing. In practice, well…

The problem is that creativity implies novelty and change. Research into this issue has found that people claim to adore creativity—until they detect an element of uncertainty. Then, they aren't just bothered by it. They get offended by it. Consciously, they may not realize their strong aversion to novel ideas. However, in studies, when given a list of positive or negative words, many people, when they sensed uncertainty in the idea, associated the new idea with words such as "vomit." Not a correlation you'd like with your next big creative concept.[13]

That's in the corporate world, where companies live or die based on innovation. But the same thing happens in schools.

98% of teachers routinely say that creativity is important. Yet almost the same number, when tested, favor less innovative children over their more creative peers.[14] Whether it is their co-workers or the children they teach, most people prefer to deal with compliant, orderly individuals who think like them and obey the rules.

With the Church, the situation is similar. It is the rare congregation that embraces true creativity, innovation, or the people who evidence those traits. Why? First, there's the perception, particularly in more conservative churches, that change means a compromise of core biblical beliefs. Or worse, they maintain a "that's not how we do it here" mindset. Second, many churches and congregations take a "two-part" view of the Bible. They see Scripture as being about the Fall and Redemption. They miss a more complete "four-part" view that includes Creation, Fall, Redemption, and Restoration. Most of our work as creative people relates more to the bookend parts of Creation and Restoration. Take those out of the story and you see why our value diminishes in the eyes of some.[15] Finally, most creatives just look and act differently. As Kevin Ashton notes in *How to Fly a Horse*:

> …people who are more creative also tend to be more playful, unconventional, and unpredictable, and all of this makes them harder to control. No matter how much we say we value creation, deep down, most of us value control more. And so we fear change and favor familiarity. Rejecting is a reflex.[16]

PARADOX AND CREATIVE CHARACTERISTICS

It is also difficult for most people to embrace paradox. And yet paradox lies at the heart of the Gospels (e.g., lose your life to gain it). It is also a key defining characteristic of creative people. In his extensive research on creative types, Mihaly Csikszentmihalyi found they exhibited ten common seemingly contradictory traits. Here's my paraphrased summary of his research:

Creative people have a lot of energy but can also rest; they can be very savvy and yet naïve or childlike; they combine playfulness but also discipline; they easily jump between reality and fantasy; they can be both introverted and extraverted, humble and proud, rebellious and conservative; they exhibit strengths of both genders; they can be both passionate and objective about their work; and their openness and sensitivity makes them more vulnerable to pain but also to greater enjoyment.[17]

If some or many of these don't sound like you, don't worry. Creative people come in all varieties. I find these paradoxical traits helpful primarily as a reminder that in The Creative Wild, a both/and mindset is the optimal approach. In most other contexts (just look at the headlines these days), you'll see we live in an either/or world. People can get downright fearful of anything that isn't black and white. As such, people find it easier to pigeonhole and label you, to make you fit their stereotypes and images. But as the list shows, that doesn't work well for creative people who evidence contradictory dimensions. We are both/and people who don't fit into most either/or environments easily. And unfortunately, this can be true within the Church as well.

IDEOLOGY AND IMAGINATION

I love the Church and see it as Plan A for Jesus' work in this world. But I also recognize how a kind of rigidity can take hold. This is particularly the case in some Evangelical circles. I realize that the term "Evangelical" has become politicized and confused in recent years. Thus, I'm referring to the more historic definition of Evangelicalism as a faith tradition that holds the Bible in great esteem.

Honoring God's Word is a great thing. However, like anything, how you do that can have unintentional consequences. With its emphasis on Scripture, Evangelicalism has, as Gregory Wolfe notes in *Beauty Will Save the World,* elevated ideology over imagination. I once read an article addressing why Evangelicals make such terrible movies. To be fair, the article is at least eight years old, and the situation is improving. But back then, the author concluded that because we are "people of the Word," we use words to convey all our meaning. And yet, film is a visual medium. Which is why a Jewish filmmaker like Steven Spielberg, or a Catholic one like Terrence Malick, makes more sophisticated films. They come from faith traditions that embrace imagery and imagination. In addition, for many Evangelical Christians, the whole point of film or any art is to make a point. Why create art that doesn't have a clear moral message?

Wolfe, however, notes this:

All great Christian art is incarnational because art itself is the act of uniting form and content, drama and idea, the medium and the message. If art is dominated by a moralistic desire to preach at the audience, it will become lifeless and didactic… Art does not work through propositions, but through the indirect, 'between the lines' means used by the imagination. We need look no further than the Gospels to be reminded of this fact. Christ's parables are marvels of compressed literary art: they employ irony, humor, satire, and paradox to startle us into a new understanding of our relationship to God. If we are too quick to boil these unsettling stories down to one-dimensional morals, they will no longer detonate in our hearts with the power that Jesus poured into them.[18]

Or to paraphrase an illustration from artist Makoto Fujimura in his book, *Art + Faith*, we are exceptionally good at explaining the laws of aerodynamics but cannot convey the sheer joy that a hawk feels when it soars.[19]

THE ROLE OF CHRISTIAN CREATIVES

When Martin Luther talked about calling, he not only upended centuries of traditions with his point that the milkmaid can serve God in her calling as well as the priest. He also gave us this illustration: Luther said that a Christian cobbler doesn't serve God better by sewing crosses on the shoes he makes. He does so by making the best pair of shoes possible. It's an indirect way of proclaiming the Gospel. And in today's world, that can be the more effective approach.

We can't argue people into the Kingdom. Rarely does that work in our society where defenses are high, and outrage is the go-to emotion. But we can *show* them that our lives are different and that the difference is Jesus. Not by sewing crosses on an inferior product but by making superior products that can become, in the words of author Alan Noble, a "disruptive witness" to the usual. This doesn't deny the Great Commission or say there's not a place—a great need, in fact—for apologetics and a clear articulation of the Good News. It says that we need a both/and posture where we also seek fresh ways of making Jesus known.

To do this requires a shift in mindset. It means recognizing there's value in appreciating the joy a hawk feels soaring. Or to realize we often gain greater insights into God through a more creative approach. As poet Christian Wiman puts it:

The purpose of theology—the purpose of any thinking about God—is to make the silences clearer and starker to us, to make the unmeaning—by which I mean those aspects of the divine that will not be reduced to human meanings—more irreducible and more terrible, and thus ultimately more wonderful. This is why art is so often better at theology than theology is.[20]

THE OPPORTUNITY TO BE A BRIDGE

Remember how I told you that the positive aspects of culture and environment were to come? Well, here they are.

You and I live in a tough environment as people of faith who are called to create. And while some on the right will see you as compromising and some on the left will see you as hanging on to outdated patriarchal notions, you have a unique opportunity. You live between two cultures. On one side, you face a secular culture that thinks you're naïve or deranged for believing in this Jesus fellow. And on the other, a traditional Christian culture that thinks you're watering down the Gospel with this art stuff. Thus, you can feel the squeeze and feel somewhat lonely. But remember this…

You and I, as creatives and members of the Body of Christ, have that paradoxical ability to live with ambiguity, tension, and not knowing. You can thus cross boundaries easier than others. You understand that all the efforts at social justice without the underlying truth of the Gospel will only change surface issues. And you appreciate that in today's world, you may best communicate truth—and have it absorbed—in an indirect form, through an image, rap lyric, or poem. That can be the best way to break through built-up defenses and touch people in unexpected ways around our common humanity.

Thus, you can see the environment in which you currently operate as a challenge and give up in fear or frustration. Or you can see that same challenge and embrace it as the reason God has given you the gifts, skills, and opportunities you have. Part of this means realizing you don't have to do this alone. Not only abiding with God as you create, but finding fellow creative believers who can support you (and you them) as you mutually strive to be faithful and create adventurously.

I sometimes lose sight of that last point. In fact, one day, while getting out of my car at the gym, I despaired that there were so few other believing creatives in this space between cultures with me. I was whining to God about feeling like Elijah in 1 Kings 9:13-18 where the prophet complained he was the only real follower of God left. And what did God do for Elijah? He told him there were 7,000 people in Israel who had never bowed down to Baal. And what did God do for me? He showed me two bumper stickers on the car next to mine. Together, they tell a message I need to remember each day, no matter what environment I'm in.

The first one on the rear window said, "Trust Jesus." Then I looked down at the bumper and read the second: "We are everywhere."

QUESTIONS AND EXPLORATIONS
- What environments have you found to be most supportive of your specific form of creativity? Least? Has anything you've read here so far helped you in thinking of ways to better navigate the less supportive environments?
- How did you react to those two bumper stickers of "Trust Jesus" and "We are Everywhere"? Do you ever feel alone as a creative believer? What might be ways to engage with others with similar interests and beliefs?
- Do you agree we can't argue people into a belief? If that's the case, what have you found to be the most effective way to share your faith? How has your creativity played a role in that or how might it?

CHAPTER 6
NAVIGATING THE CREATIVE WILD

Where you learn what the creative process is, why bad advice can be so devastating, the importance of tools over rules, and how and when to trust your intuition and God's leading.

When I face the desolate impossibility of writing five hundred pages, a sick sense of failure falls on me, and I know I can never do it. Then gradually, I write one page and then another. One day's work is all I can permit myself to contemplate.
— John Steinbeck, *Travels with Charley: In Search of America*

It's not wise to violate the rules until you know how to observe them.
— T.S. Eliot

Before you can think out of the box, you have to start with a box.
— Twyla Tharp, *The Creative Habit*

If mindset, motivation, mastery, and a supportive environment are the *essentials* everyone needs to create adventurously, what follows are more like optional personal preferences or approaches for navigating The Creative Wild. Some people prefer a roadmap. Others like rules or guidelines. Still others rely on intuition built through experience. The only right way to make it through The Creative Wild is the way that works for you. And while there are likely more approaches to do this than there are embarrassing dance videos on TikTok, let's explore these three approaches—roadmap, rules, and intuition—so that you can decide the right combination for your own explorations.

KNOW THE OVERALL PROCESS

Defining the creative process as a roadmap for making is like saying that an atlas of the United States is a roadmap for your road trip through Ohio. The atlas points out the major highways and landmarks, but there are a lot of details it leaves out. Still, the following version of what we know about the creative process can at least alert you to the common milestones and directions. I've found it helpful because I've heard for so long to "trust the process," but I was never clear what that process was. So here it is.

There have been many variations on the process that Graham Wallace first laid out in 1926 as the four stages of Preparation, Incubation, Illumination, and Verification. What I'm sharing here summarizes my favorite. I like it because it avoids the weakness of many of the versions of the creative process that focus mostly on ideation. As we'll see, I believe that ideation without execution is not much different from daydreaming. Everyone has ideas. Creators make them real.

The following version of the creative process comes from *The Universal Traveler*.[21] I've used their version as a starting point and have changed it based on research since it was written, as well as my experience. Normally, I'm a fan of lists and labels. But because the creative process is, well, creative, and more of a general approach than a defined step-by-step guide, I'm going to summarize it in lay terms.

First, you figure out with any creative endeavor if it is worth doing. You get ready. You then research the issue to know what others have done and what the related elements might be. Next, you define what the real problem is you're trying to solve. As we'll see, this is probably the most important step and the one most people miss because they focus on symptoms instead of root issues. Once you know the problem, you let it rest and incubate. This is the stage where you're in the shower, say, and an answer appears out of nowhere. It's because your brain has been stewing on it in the background during this phase. You then move into the idea generation phase (where quantity counts most) and then to the idea evaluation phase (where quality is your goal). Once you select the best option to pursue, you experiment with different prototypes and possibilities. Eventually, you produce the final product and share it with others. The final step is to then evaluate and learn from all these previous steps.

I call this a roadmap, but the creation process is rarely this linear, particularly with more improvisational forms of creativity, and you can often loop through the stages like a corkscrew. You may also find that the Implementation phase, where you actually make something, is by far the most involved. But I find it encouraging to know there is a process that most creatives go through. It's also useful to remind me of steps I may not have considered. But it is not a formula. As I note elsewhere, you won't find formulas or step-by-step recipes either in the Bible or in The Creative Wild.

But what if you want something a little less nebulous just to give you confidence you're doing this whole creating thing right? That's when you can turn to our second option: rules.

FOLLOW THE RIGHT RULES

Every creative area has their own rules or guidelines. The Chicago and AP style guides give us rules of good writing. We have various principles in design like the Golden Mean, or, in photography, the Rule of Thirds. Novelists have plotting structures and tropes. Woodworkers have simple heuristics such as "measure twice, cut once." In cooking, there are prescribed ways to fluff your egg whites or proof your bread.

Knowing these rules is like learning techniques. They can be transformative when they help and a roadblock when they don't. The problem is, how do you know which rules to follow and which to ignore? Before I answer, let me expand on the danger of following rules without careful consideration.

Rules are, in some ways, unformed habits imposed on us by others. Even if we say we hate rules and resist all advice, some of it seeps through—unless you're still hiding in a cave waiting out the aftermath of Y2K. Even the most rebellious of creators may still cling to tips and techniques tossed to them like life preservers when they're not sure what to do. It's much easier to follow someone else's directions than to navigate our own way through a new situation. We figure, "Hey, at least they've done this before. That's more than me. Even if their advice is only somewhat helpful, it's better than none."

That would be true except for this: Once we accept a piece of advice, we're often the ones who convert it into a rule. Rather than go through the discomfort of not knowing, we adhere to that piece of advice and make it our own. When counter options come our way, we ignore them or worse, defend what we've picked up as if it is the only way. We value experimentation when we feel secure. We want the comfort of directions from others when we're not.

Besides perfectionism, few things will hamper your journey through The Creative Wild like bad advice. Bad advice can make you question your unique approach to creativity and lead you in unhelpful directions. And again, that advice may not be universally bad, like a mullet or a polyester leisure suit. Just bad for you or for this moment or for this project. Even guidelines that worked for you before may not work now. Thus, it helps to hold such rules lightly and to question them all. Even the ones in this book.

So, back to the earlier question: How do you know what rules to follow? In the same way you discover your callings and life purpose: through experimentation.

TEST DRIVE THE ADVICE YOU GET

"You can't break the rules until you know the rules." It's a familiar refrain. But neither can you ignore them unless you understand them enough. Some so-called rules just won't be a fit. You'll know this immediately based on what we'll soon cover regarding your intuition. For example, when I first heard that real writers forgo all other creative outlets and concentrate only on the craft of writing, I assumed it was true. It didn't align with my own sensibilities or limited experience, but what did I know? I didn't, at the time, have any countervailing input, and the source of this advice seemed trustworthy.

While that advice may have worked for that person and for many others, I later learned that only 20% of people in the US do their best work when focused on one area. A whopping 65% of us do better creative work when we have multiple creative areas going, say, writing, choreography, ceramics, and cooking.[22]

I should have listened to my intuition on this advice, but I thought I'd try it out. Thus, I attempted to focus only on writing for some time and let other creative interests lag. What I discovered was that my writing suffered. But still assuming the advice was true, I figured I'd just work harder and focus more.

Experimentation ended up revealing what my intuition already knew, but that I ignored: I need multiple creative streams in my life to excel in any of them. So again, test all "rules" and see what works for you. Some you'll immediately reject. Some you'll discard after they no longer serve you or your context changes. And some you'll use for the rest of your life. Just like a good tool.

TRUST YOUR INSTINCTS

Now let's look more closely at the third approach to navigating The Creative Wild, the role of intuition.

I recently read *Dear Writer, Are You Intuitive?* by Becca Syme and Susan Bichoff. I found it liberating because it provided validation for trusting my intuition in so many areas of my creative life. If you have areas where you "just know" the right way forward but can't explain how you know, it's likely you have a strong sense of intuition in that area.

The challenge for intuitive writers or creatives is that not everyone is intuitive in the same way or area. There are multiple types of intuition and, as with spiritual gifts, no one person has all types. And for those who differ from you or haven't developed their intuition, they won't understand you or your method. They'll wonder why you're not following their approaches or the "rules" that "everyone knows" are the "right way" to do things.

It can take a lot of courage to hold to your convictions when people ask you for the data to prove your position. You won't have that data. At least not in a handy spreadsheet. But you've accumulated information over time and have internalized it. You're not just guessing. You're basing your decisions on a lifetime of stored up input.

Eventually, you learn where to trust your instincts and where to rely on guidelines and advice from others. For example, with color selection, my intuition is as sharp as a bowling ball. But put me in a room where my branding clients are spewing forth tagline ideas, and out of hundreds, when I hear a good one, it's like my Spidey Senses kick in and I just know that one will work.

Be careful not to fall into the common trap of believing that because your instincts are spot-on in one area, your opinions will be right in others. Learn to trust your intuition only in areas where it's proven to be right. After all, being correct and feeling certain aren't the same. Strive for where they align.

I tend not to share this intuitive approach with anyone but a trusted few because either they won't get it, or it will encourage others who don't have the same developed instincts to act as if they do. Then we just get into an opinion fest. But for you, when evaluating what advice or direction to follow, heed your gut and your spirit.

If all this sounds rather vague, just try explaining how God speaks to you. I think much of our intuition relates to the Holy Spirit's work in our life. You know it. You just can't explain it.

TOOLS NOT RULES

Let's bring this all together. To navigate The Creative Wild, I think the best way is to combine all these approaches. Be aware of the creative process. Listen to new advice, but test it to see what works for you. Then let your instincts and the Holy Spirit guide you.

Beyond that, consider adopting a mindset of "tools not rules." Instead of treating the advice you hear as a rule to follow, treat it as a tool (or approach, method, principle, technique—whatever term works for you) to use. I like "tools" because it implies something you use for a given purpose. Plus, it rhymes better with "rules." As an example, when researching the concept of beauty for this book, I found so many definitions of it as to render it meaningless. Like intuition, you recognize beauty but can't explain it. Then I came across an insight in John-Mark L. Miravalle's book *Beauty: What It Is And Why It Matters*. He doesn't define beauty so much as point out two characteristics of it, order and surprise. This has been a brilliant aid to me because I now realize how many things I thought were beautiful, were merely decorative. They either lacked a pleasing sense of order or were as surprising as rush hour. Still, I don't make order and surprise into a rule. But I find it a very helpful tool for evaluating if my work evidences both when I'm striving to make something beautiful.

In the same way, the remaining chapters in this book are more tools than rules for creating adventurously. Some will be more relevant at some times than others, but all are vital in doing creative work. As you read through the following chapters that explain these tools, sense which ones resonate most at this point. Try each one out. Experiment. Strive to incorporate them into your practice and find fresh approaches on how and when to use them. Abide with Jesus as you make, and trust that he will guide you as to which tool to use when.

Now let's turn to those tools starting with the first one, Readiness.

QUESTIONS AND EXPLORATIONS

- How do you react to the idea that two of the key criteria of beauty are order and surprise? How might you use these in a specific project?
- Look back at the creative process I've outlined. Which phases of that do you find most enjoyable? Which are stressful? For the latter, make a conscious list of what stresses you and why (as much as you can tell). Just naming your concerns helps to diminish them. Then use your creativity to come up with a list of new ways you might go about each phase.
- Think of some advice or a so-called rule that you've followed without questioning it. How has that gone? For ones that didn't work out, how long did you go before abandoning or altering the "rule?" How can you be more discerning in the future on what advice you accept or not?

PART III

Tools for Creating Adventurously

In which the hero (you), is granted access to the creative mindset tools that will enable you to get unstuck, create more adventurously, do better creative work, and find deeper satisfaction in making and life.

READINESS: *OVERVIEW OF THE BOXES*

Between each of the following chapters, you'll find a page with a photo of a box. This wooden box, 2' x 2' square and eight inches deep, remains the same throughout, but the contents in the box change to align with one of my creative interests. Each interest, in turn, relates to the chapter that follows.

I first became aware of the idea of "box art" with the work of Joseph Cornell. I'd always felt an affinity for boxes. They are inherently mysterious. There's usually an element of anticipation as well before you open one. And they can be as prosaic as a banker's box of old files and as captivating as a treasure chest.

Boxes are containers for our lives, literally and figuratively. And as a symbol, they remind us of how great art—really, most creativity—flourishes within limits. I found the restrictions of using the same box to be both constraining and liberating. Using one box instilled consistency. However, through the repetition of the same container, I became freer to experiment with the content.

I've never done collage work like this before. I loved the combination of composition and improvisation involved. I also like the results that you'll see. But I realize now how much further I could have thought "outside the box" and pushed each one to become more of a showpiece of a different world rather than an interesting (hopefully) arrangement of thematic objects. But that is the beauty of The Creative Wild and creating as an act of grace. There is always tomorrow and a chance to re-create the work in new ways.

For more on the making of these boxes, go to http://www.exploreyourworlds.com/boxes or use this QR code:

CHAPTER 7
READINESS

Where you realize you have more assets and agency than you thought, so you can prepare for what lies ahead in The Creative Wild.

———————

I don't know who you are. I don't know what you want. If you are looking for ransom, I can tell you I don't have money, but what I do have are a very particular set of skills. Skills I have acquired over a very long career. Skills that make me a nightmare for people like you. If you let my daughter go now, that'll be the end of it. I will not look for you, I will not pursue you, but if you don't, I will look for you, I will find you and I will kill you.

— Liam Neeson, **Taken**

You too have skills. Maybe not as lethal or dramatic as those in this scene from the movie, *Taken*. But vital in their own way. The challenge is to understand what they are, know how to use them, and then prepare yourself for applying them. This is the work of Readiness.

We lead off our review of the tools for creating adventurously with Readiness because it's what you need when you're starting in a new creative area. But it is also something you carry with you and use throughout your creative life.

Readiness means being always prepared for creative possibilities. Sometimes that's just being alert amid other activities. Other times, it's creating intentional space and time for making.

Readiness is not just about preparing for a particular creative project. It's about preparing you for any creative project. It's an alertness to the Holy Spirit and how he can guide you in all your creative work.

READY FOR WHAT?

Readiness involves actively seeking what interests you. Because you want to do something with what you discover, you could say this: *Readiness is curiosity expressed in action.*

At the start of a project, I often ask, "Is this project worth the time, effort, heartache, and love it will take?" Those and other factors can make determining what project to work on a complex calculus. But I can simplify the decision when I focus on this point about interest.

If my desire is strong enough, I don't let a lack of time, skills, experience, or other issues get in the way. While market forces or opportunities matter, most often for me, it comes down to desire. William Kenower addresses this well regarding writers:

When I ask, 'What can I write that will put me on the bestseller list?' I am asking myself to predict the future. I am saying, 'Don't bother starting something until you know it will succeed.' I can't know that, and I never will. But I do know what I'm interested in and curious about…In fact, I would say the greatest difference between the professional writers I know and those just embarking on their writing journey is that the professional writer understands that she needs only her authentic interest in a story or an idea to know it is worthy of her full attention. The beginning writer often doubts this. He thinks, Everyone's curious about something. What makes my curiosity so special? And what if no one else is interested in what I'm interested in?[23]

READINESS AND DOING THE WORK

That initial interest may get me started, but Readiness helps me prepare myself, my tools, materials, space, and other people to sustain me through the process. When I do this preparation well, there's a greater likelihood of something amazing happening down the road. I till the soil and plant the seeds and then look expectantly to what God will do with this. I don't kick back and drink Mojitos in the shade, hoping the crop will come in. I'm still weeding and watering. I'm an active co-creator in all of this. But I do so with this sense of anticipation, hope, and faith that good will come of it all. Even—or maybe especially—if I don't feel qualified for doing the work before me.

Madeleine L'Engle addresses so well the challenge of Readiness, the simultaneous sense of not being equipped or qualified for the task at hand, and the ongoing practice that makes us ready:

There's a paradox here, and a trap for the lazy. I do not need to be 'qualified' to play a Bach fugue on the piano…But I cannot play that Bach fugue at all if I do not play the piano daily, if I do not practice my finger exercises. There are equivalents of finger exercises in the writing of books, the painting of portraits, the composing of a song. We do not need to be qualified; the gift is free; and yet we have to pay for it.[24]

COUNTING YOUR ASSETS

This preparation for entering—and staying ready in—The Creative Wild starts with an accurate assessment of what you have and what you're up against. Let's begin with the former.

When I worked for the international humanitarian organization, World Vision, I learned of an approach known as Asset-Based Community Development (ABCD). This model acknowledges that every neighborhood or community, no matter how challenged they may appear, has assets. These are often not obvious. While the community may lack good schools, outside investment, maintained infrastructure, or healthy food options, they have assets of relationships, networks, history in the place, under-used buildings and real estate, local knowhow, and an awareness of how to get things done there. Once the community realizes their collective assets, transformation can occur. Instead of outside "experts" coming in and telling them what they need, they can determine this for themselves, and, through collective action, do something about it.

This same ABCD approach applies to you. You likely have assets you aren't even aware of. Or if you are, you may discount them, assuming they are of little value. Or maybe you realize their worth, but do not know how to activate or leverage them. In the same way that many economically challenged communities assume that since they lack monetary assets, they are poor, so too you might assume that since you lack certain resources (skills, talent, economic freedom to do your art, experience, capital, connections to influencers, materials, access, exposure, a fan base, etc.) you don't have what it takes to succeed. But the beauty of the ABCD model is that sometimes, the least obvious assets become the most powerful. And once you identify your assets, it becomes like Mary Poppins' carpet bag, where all kinds of surprises emerge.

When you realize how many of the hurdles facing you creatively are mindset related more than physical, you can shift from focusing on what you don't have to what you do. And what do you have?

Take a moment right now to consider and write a starting list of your creative assets. These could include:
- networks
- your upbringing
- life experiences
- a positive perspective
- grit
- supportive family and friends
- time
- praise for past work

- excellent hand-eye coordination
- tools
- your sense of humor
- mentors
- a keen sense of rhythm or balance
- access to a good working space
- ways of thinking that differ from others
- little tips and techniques you've absorbed in a variety of areas
- sound theology
- strong faith
- counselors
- ingenuity
- the willingness to work hard
- friends of friends
- your ability to hold your breath
- drawing a perfect circle
- knowing when an instrument is out of tune, etc.

Jot down any physical attributes that can help. Same with aids to your mindset and motivation. Note how many of these apply beyond the "artistic" realm. You can use these assets—and any others you can think of—for problem solving and creative efforts in any area of life.

GROWING YOUR SENSE OF AGENCY

One of your greatest assets will be a sense of personal agency. Agency relates to how much control you feel you have over your thoughts, actions, and situations. Agency grows when you see your actions make a difference. This is why I emphasize experimentation so much in this book. The more you try different approaches, the more you see the correlation between cause and effect. When you see that your efforts and the choices you made work out, your agency grows.

You also realize how much lies outside your control. That's important too, since it helps to differentiate the situations we have to leave to God and those we can change. Far too many of the things that stress me in life lie outside my control. Realizing this, turning those things over to God, and focusing on what I can control has made a dramatic difference in my ability to create adventurously.

As I do so, I'm building my courage, confidence, and *capacity* for trying other new things. We often think we must have courage before we try something new. In reality, it's more the opposite. John O'Donohue notes in his book *Beauty*:

It is courage that restores hope to the heart. In our day to day lives, we often show courage without realizing it. However, it is only when we are afraid that courage becomes a question. Courage is amazing because it can tap into the heart of fear, taking that frightened energy and turning towards initiative, creativity, action and hope. When courage comes alive, imprisoning walls become frontiers of new possibility, difficulty becomes invitation and the heart comes into a new rhythm of trust and sureness.[25]

You may think that the nemesis of courage is fear. And it can be. But in The Creative Wild, a particular form of fear shows up far too often. It can mess with your sense of Readiness more than just about anything else. What makes it so insidious is that most of us don't even think of it as fear. We write it off as an idiosyncrasy or bad habit. But it still stems from fear. And its name—cue the serious, "bad guys are coming" music—is perfectionism.

THE CHALLENGE OF PERFECTIONISM

Over and over, I hear from creators how debilitating perfectionism is to their creativity. This applies to both those who never start because they feel they couldn't do the work perfectly and those who never finish, for many of the same reasons. Leonardo Da Vinci, one of history's poster children for perfectionism, never completed his painting, *The Adoration of the Magi*. This was in part because, polymath that he was, ol' Leo was studying the science of optics around the same time as he worked on the painting. And because of that, he realized he could never figure out—perfectly—how light reflected off the faces of the over 30 individuals in the scene.[26]

When I recently saw the work at the Uffizi Gallery in Florence, Italy, I was so impressed by the composition and other details, even in their unfinished state, that I didn't care if Leonardo got the angles of reflected light perfect. But he did. Which explains why we have less than 20 existing paintings that are accepted as his but thousands of pages of his notes (where perfectionism didn't get in the way).

Perfectionism, a bad thing, is deadly because it comes so close to pursuing excellence, a good thing. You want to work to the best of your abilities. But you are human, not a machine. As such, you'll never achieve a creative work without some flaw, some minor imperfection. That's not a limitation. That's a plus. It's what keeps you grounded and authentic. As Artificial Intelligence (AI) duplicates more and more of what we creators can do, it is your human quirks that will make your work inimitable and stand out.

When we talk about the value of imperfection in creative work, it doesn't mean you pursue mistakes. It means that few things ever go as planned. If you see each detour from the intended outcome as an interesting creative twist, you'll make a better creative product. If you see it as a mistake or failure, you won't last long in The Creative Wild.

In their wonderful book on this subject, *Art & Fear: Observations on the Perils (and Rewards) of Artmaking*, David Bayles and Ted Orland note that:

> *…imperfection is not only a common ingredient in art, but very likely an essential ingredient. Ansel Adams, never one*

to mistake precision for perfection, often recalled the old adage that 'the perfect is the enemy of the good', his point being that if he waited for everything in the scene to be exactly right, he'd probably never make a photograph.[27]

You won't be able to maintain a state of readiness if you're consumed with some unattainable ideal about what you or your work should be. Far better to dive in and try than stand outside The Creative Wild waiting for the optimal conditions. Readiness is about that willingness to jump in at any moment and to do whatever you can, right now, perfect or not.

CREATIVE CHANGE MANAGEMENT

Readiness is also about embracing change. This is easier to do when you're the one orchestrating it. To do so well, I've found it helpful, even on a personal level, to use a formula for change management associated with large organizations. Yes, I know I said there are no formulas in The Creative Wild. But as you'll see, this is more a framework than a formula. As best as I can determine, Dr. Mary Lippett developed it in 1987. It looks like this:

MANAGING COMPLEX CHANGE

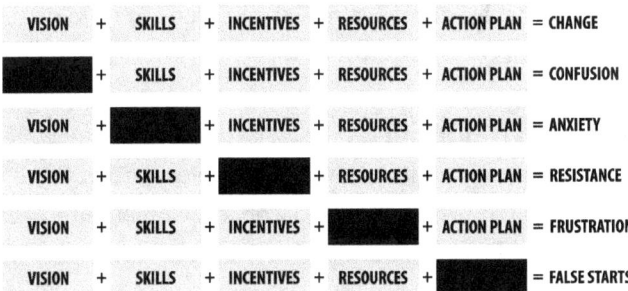

If you have Vision+Skills+Incentives+Resources+an Action Plan, then you get Change. Build up each of those elements just a little, you tip the scales toward achieving that Change. But if you are missing any one of these keys, the outcome will be either Confusion, Anxiety, Resistance, Frustration or False Starts. For example, I may have Skills, Incentives, Resources, and an Action Plan, but without Vision, I'm going to spin and wonder what I'm even trying to do.

With Vision, you need just enough of a sense of a preferred outcome to get you going. With Skills, remember you need both subject-specific skills and creativity/mindset skills. With Incentives, we're back to desire and your overarching motivation to create. With Resources, those could be time, money, help, or any of the assets we looked at previously. And for an Action Plan, as with Vision, it just needs to be detailed enough to provide an outline of the tasks you'll undertake.

To me, the formula helps by breaking down the unknowns and focusing me on what I should work on. You need not (unless that's your jam) try to articulate every step of the change management formula for each project, especially for smaller ones. But, as with the creative process, just having a sense of each component can help you with Readiness.

Like the old line about how a good plan executed today is better than the best plan executed tomorrow, don't wait until you have what you think are the optimal levels of each of the components here. Because you never will. Waiting is just another form of perfectionism, or at least procrastination (they tend to go to the same clubs and parties).

YOUR MOST VITAL ASSET

This formula or framework won't guarantee success. But it will help you narrow down what steps to work on. Combine it and abiding with the Holy Spirit, and you're well on your way to Readiness. Doing both helps you disarm perfectionism, alerts you to your key assets and sense of agency, focuses you on the Person not the problem, and helps you create in grace. Most of all, when you abide, God will remind you that Readiness is a state, not an end. You don't have to figure everything out ahead of time. He'll show you—usually in indirect and often surprising ways—the next step. And the next. And if not, if you're not getting clear direction, you can trust that he's still with you no matter what. He's not a GPS app dictating each next turn so much as the best kind of traveling companion, one who is content to just be with you even if they say nothing.

There's a passage, Joshua 3:5, that I'm going to take out of context here. That's not normally a good practice, but bear with me. Joshua said these words to the Israelites the day before they crossed the River Jordan into the Promised Land. But I think it works for us adventurous creatives as well. It could be our slogan for Readiness, every single day: "Consecrate yourselves, for tomorrow the LORD will do amazing things among you." And he will. The question is this: Are you ready?

QUESTIONS AND EXPLORATIONS

- How might this quote help you start a project or overcome perfectionism? "Even in literature and art, no man who bothers about originality will ever be original: whereas if you simply try to tell the truth (without caring two pence how often it has been told before) you will, nine times out of ten, become original without ever having noticed it." — C. S. Lewis, *Mere Christianity*
- Counting your assets helps most in the areas where you think you have few. For many of us, this is in marketing and selling our work. We think we need to know tactics and advertising approaches. But what helps is knowing people. Make a list of as many people you know or know of, outlets related to them (podcasts, websites, stories, galleries, markets and fairs, etc.), friends of friends, networks, or other connections you have. For each person, think about how they could help you and how you might bless them.
- Think of a time when you felt ready for some event or activity. What did you do that made you feel ready? How could you take what you learned and apply it to your next project?

RHYTHM: *MUSIC*

When I was around four, I would stand by the piano as my grandmother taught my brother how to play. His interest in the instrument soon waned, but mine only increased. By the time I was five, I was the one getting the lessons. They continued with different teachers for the next twelve years.

In college, I was going to be a music minor. I had a strong background in theory and had always played well by ear. And then I met Dave Griswald. He later became a concert pianist (and a good friend). But I remember the day when I realized he could not only play by ear better than me, but he could sight-read a piece of music for the first time and play it better than I could after practicing that piece for a month. I switched minors.

My love for music, both playing and composing, however, has remained, even if it is only for fun. When I am spiritually stuck, few things reconnect me to God, like music. And the deeper understanding of rhythm, pacing, rests, volume, harmony, and so much more has enhanced all my other creative efforts in so many ways.

Music is also for me, one of the most mysterious of the creative areas I enjoy. 19th century German philosopher Arthur Schopenhauer considered music to be the greatest art form because, unlike painting or literature, music doesn't represent something else.[28] Many, since then, have echoed his sentiment about the purity of music and its ability to transport us in ways both powerful and inexplicable. Like sleep, we know we need it, but no one can explain exactly how music affects us the way it does.

It reminds me of just how much we are guided by rhythms in our lives that go beyond our understanding. So, the next time you need a bit more mystery and awe in your life, look up to the heavens on a clear night—and listen to the music.

CHAPTER 8
RHYTHM

Where you discover and attune to the cadence, patterns, energy modes, and routines that work best for you.

Now this is very profound, what rhythm is, and goes far deeper than words. A sight, an emotion, creates this wave in the mind, long before it makes words to fit it ...
— Virginia Woolf

In the shapeliness of a life, habit plays its sovereign role.
— Mary Oliver, **Long Life: Essays and Other Writings**

Time is the raw material of creation... Creating consumes. It is all day, every day. It knows neither weekends nor vacations. It is not when we feel like it. It is habit, compulsion, obsession, and vocation. The common thread that links creators is how they spend their time.
— Kevin Ashton, **How to Fly a Horse**

Every successful creative person ultimately discovers a rhythm or cadence that suits them alone. For many professionals, it means showing up at the same time in the same space each day. But that regularity doesn't work for everyone.

One of the most freeing moments in my creative life was the day I realized that just because a daily schedule works for many creatives, it doesn't mean it fits my rhythm. Ironically, once I gave myself permission to move beyond an every day requirement, I found I thrived on some daily practices such as early morning writing.

Others adhere to consistent schedules but are less picky about location. Some are the opposite: They need to work in the same space each day, but they vary the hours. Others still are more opportunistic and take advantage of getting up early, commute time, or sitting in the car during their kid's soccer practice to get creative work done.

One of my favorite examples of this flexibility in rhythms comes from when I was in college and worked as a magician at Disneyland. As part of my training in the Disney way, I got to visit the famed Imagineers, the designers and engineers who worked on new rides at the theme parks. What impressed me most wasn't just their creativity, but their work schedule. This was back in an era when few people worked from home and flexible schedules were as common then as flexible opinions are now. They were regularly given an assignment and a deadline of, say, six weeks. They could choose their schedule, as long as they made the deadline.

Some would immediately dive in, working evenings and weekends and finish two weeks before the deadline, then go on vacation. Others did the opposite, dawdling until the deadline loomed large, then working almost non-stop for the last week to finish on time. Still others kept bankers' hours through the entire project. In short, few of them did it the same way or with the same rhythms. That should encourage you to pursue the creative rhythm that works best for you.

For me, I prefer focusing on flexible practices over fixed routines. I still build the habits and even systems that nurture consistent work, just not in a locked-down manner. But that's me. You'll only learn what works for you time-wise through experimentation. And through realizing that all time is not the same.

SPEND MORE TIME IN THE RIGHT TIME

The adage that you overestimate what you can do in a day and underestimate what you can do in a year shows how little we grasp time. As creatives, we love to get lost in the feeling of flow where we lose all track of time. But that flow state is really more about controlled consciousness than time.[29] When you select your focus and enter flow, you shift time from this scarce resource you must manage to this state where time doesn't register. And once freed from the tyranny of the clock, you can explore aspects of your work on a much richer level. The result? You have more of the right time to make something beautiful.

As I explored in *Hidden Travel,* the ancient Greeks had two different words for time. *Chronos* refers to linear, clock time, a quantitative measurement. *Kairos* is qualitative and non-linear, tracked in moments, seasons, and opportunities. "What time is the party?" is a *chronos* question. "Did you have a good time at the party?" is a *kairos* one.

Productivity hacks are like catnip to *chronos*. You can't escape *chronos* (as the crow's feet around the eyes attest). Appointments and obligations don't disappear. But you can spend—or make—more time in *kairos*. There, you realize that creative output isn't tied to a clock, and that flow doesn't happen if you're constantly checking your watch.

Want better ideas? Enter *kairos* and let yourself daydream or be bored. Use divergent thinking to make unlikely connections that spur fresher ideas. Leverage *chronos* for convergent thinking that refines and prioritizes those ideas for execution.

Chronos and *kairos* may seem like opposites. However, deadlines (a classic *chronos* tool) can do wonders for creative breakthroughs. And many efficiency boosts emerge when you take *kairos* moments to find better ways to be productive. Shifting to a moment's orientation can also move you from the tyranny of *chronos* and into the freedom of *kairos*. Instead of thinking, "I only have 25 minutes until my next call," and squandering that time in distractions, think, "I have this free *moment* to create." The irony is that you'll be more productive (a *chronos* trait) by thinking of time in non-*chronos* ways.

LEVERAGING YOUR ENERGY

While understanding and even managing your time is important, even more so, for adventurous creatives, is doing the same with your energy. This starts with sensing when you're most alert and arranging your schedule, if possible, around what works best for your circadian rhythms and sleep needs. Sleep, in fact, is one of the most important and least practiced creative tools. We're a nation of chronically sleep-deprived people, and creatives are no different. I don't give a chapter to it here (mostly because so much is written about it elsewhere), but I can't stress enough its value. As the late Dallas Willard once said, "God did not create us to be tired."

Your *chronos*-related circadian rhythms will determine if you're a morning or evening person. But that's not the end of the story because your *creative* rhythms can be more flexible. For example, as a morning lark, my own circadian rhythms normally mean I'm tired in the early afternoon. Ordering my day by the clock would mean no creative work from, say, 2:00 to 4:00 pm. But that would make it a rule, and you know how I feel about those. Instead, organizing my activities by my energy or creative rhythms means that if a meeting just got canceled and I now have a block of free time, that can reignite my creative juices, even if that time slot is usually an energy tar pit for me.

Thus, rather than being a slave to *chronos* approaches, ask these questions from author David Kadavy in his book, *Mind Management Not Time Management,* each time you want to leverage *kairos* and energy over *chronos*: "What work am I in the mood to do right now?" Then, ask yourself, "What do I need to do that fits that mood?"

I used to think of moods as something to cave into or push through. Now, I see them as something to leverage because you'll do more and better creative work when you can align a specific type of work with your specific mood. For example, Kadavy notes that most people have more energy at the start of the day (unless you're a night owl). Thus, do your most creative work in the early morning, when you're groggy and your brain's prefrontal cortex (or PFC, the home to your inner "critic" voice) is still snoozing. If you're too alert, your PFC is likely to kick in and start pointing out all the faults in what you're making. You can't freely create and revise at the same time, so use this time of day for more divergent, imaginative thinking. Later, when your PFC has had its coffee and is up barking orders, use that time for editing and other more convergent types of thinking.

To be even more specific, Kadavy notes seven "mental states" that align with different moods:

- Prioritize (planning)
- Explore (connecting diverse sources, which happens when you're, say, reading articles or books on a wide range of subjects and looking for a spark or connection)
- Research (when you know the subject or reference you need to find and go hunting for it)
- Generate (the deepest level of creativity where you come up with the wild ideas without evaluating them yet)
- Polish (refine or edit)
- Administrate (doing the boring tasks—unless you love admin)
- Refresh (rest)

I'd add an eighth one for Social (including calls, meetings, or events) since for both introverts and extroverts, interactions with people will affect your energy. Whatever your categories, ordering your day by energy mode/mental state can be a breakthrough (it has for me) in helping you spend more time in creative *kairos* and less in the stress of *chronos*.

What also has helped me—and again, not just your mileage but your entire destination may vary—has been the benefit of having multiple creative interests. The regularity of the first-thing-in-the-morning Generative mode works well for me for writing and ideation. But later in the day, when I have nothing left to give to my writing (or so it feels), I may be energized to do more production-oriented work like processing photos in Lightroom or Photoshop, or stepping outside artistic areas to problem solve household issues. Thus, energy modes and types of projects work together to keep me moving forward throughout the day.

THE RHYTHM OF IDENTITY

What I'm about to describe may not seem like a rhythm. But there is a certain cadence to it over time. I'm referring to the shifting labels—a form of identity, really—of amateur and professional. Those can seem more like a progression: you start as an amateur, gain Mastery, and go pro. But it's not that neat. We've all seen many amateurs who create brilliant works that rival anything sold for money, and many professionals whose work one could only describe as amateurish. Even more, we will all be amateurs in some areas of our creative lives even as we excel and get paid for our creative work in others. The dance or rhythm occurs when you embrace—and move back and forth between—elements of both: the standards of the pro and the passion of the amateur.

The word "amateur" comes from the Latin *amare,* to love. Amateur used to mean someone who does something because they love it. Now, for many, it implies second-rate, someone whose work gets, at best, a response of "Oh, that's nice, dear." And yet, it is the zeal of the amateur that keeps many art forms alive and fresh.

With the term professional, are you a pro when you make all your income from your creative work? Part of your income?

And what about the Emily Dickinsons and Franz Kafkas who sold none of their work? Were they not professionals?

Getting paid for your creative work provides validation. It lets you focus more time and resources on that work. But the labels of "amateur" and "pro" can pigeonhole you rather than liberate. So it may help to define them less by income and more by attitude and rhythm.

To me, in the best sense, an amateur creates strictly for the joy of making. They maintain that childlike delight and hold the process lightly as a gift from God to be cherished and shared. They remember we are at our best when we do everything out of love.

Similarly, in the best sense, being a "pro" means committing not just to regular practice, but to growth, maintaining high standards, showing up when you don't feel like it, and welcoming feedback. It can mean working at a faster pace and realizing that deadlines leave no room for perfectionism or over-thinking. Your work could include hobbies, side gigs, and multiple creative interests, some paid, some not. But you are always learning and growing. You do the work for the work and the process, not the label. You don't rely on feeling inspired. You work until you are. You realize that the greater your skill and effort, the more often inspiration comes your way. As author Seth Godin puts it, "'Do what you love' is for amateurs but 'love what you do' is the mantra for professionals."[30] You discover that the secret to creating adventurously may come down to this: *Love your work like an amateur and do your work like a pro.*

The creative work I do for a living in branding and writing is satisfying and makes a difference. But the non-paid work I do in other creative areas is life-giving. That's a sentiment I feel is getting lost in today's culture that encourages you to "monetize your creativity" and "do what you love for a living." I think it's the best of both worlds when you can get paid well for your creative work. But I also know that the slower pace and even worshipful extravagance of creating simply for the joy of making has rewards that go far beyond monetary ones. With some of my creative interests, such as furniture design, when I've done it for pay, all the joy gets swept away with the sawdust. I need some creative areas of my life to stay in the amateur realm simply to fuel my inspiration and creative soul.

Most of all, I need the different rhythm of personal projects to balance the often-frenetic pace of paid work. It's like at a concert where the performers will do a skillful mix of slow and fast songs. We need that variety of rhythms in our creative lives as well.

THE VALUE OF SLOWING DOWN

The challenge is that following the slower paced rhythms isn't easy. We feel pressured to do more faster, and yet the human brain can only go as fast as our biological wiring allows. This push for speed and productivity particularly hurts our creativity by diminishing our ability to pay attention and be present. Let me give you an example from a recent trip to Italy.

One rainy evening in a small town in Puglia (the region in the boot's heel of Italy), I was chatting with the owner of a café. I commented on the square on which the café sat and noted the beauty of the white-painted walls (this area was once Greek) and the architectural details. Then, I pointed out how, even on a gloomy evening when few tourists or even locals bothered to come out, carefully placed floodlights brilliantly lit the square. I asked her, "Do you think the Italians value beauty more than the Americans?" She shook her head and replied, "No. It's not that. It's that Italians slow down enough to appreciate it. You Americans are always in a rush. But you can't appreciate this…" as she pointed to the square, "if you're in a hurry."

I think that's true whether it is in a small Italian city, the natural beauty of God's creation, the creative work of others, or our own efforts. There's a point at which our pace, if too rapid, can nullify our own creative sensibilities. Even the most adventurous of creatives needs to slow down at times. Not just to see better and focus, but to get in touch with and appreciate what God has placed all around us—all we'd miss at a faster pace.

THE GIFT OF RHYTHMS

In slowing down in my life, I realize that aligning with my creative rhythms is the difference between flow and frustration. For each of us, we'll do better work and enjoy it more when we abide, not just with Jesus, but in *kairos*. We'll get more done when we align our work with our energy modes, moods, and rhythms. We'll engage it more regularly when we love our work like an amateur, but carry it out like a pro. And we'll appreciate it all more when we slow down enough to savor it and the wonder all around us.

Few things have enhanced my creative life as much as understanding and then attuning to the right rhythms—for me, for the work I'm doing, or even for this season of life. Can I work if my creative rhythms are off? Of course. But why would I want to?

It may take you a while to appreciate the value of finding and heeding your creative rhythms. But when you do, not only does your work become easier, it becomes far more satisfying and exciting because you get in touch with a rhythm far greater than you.

QUESTIONS AND EXPLORATIONS

- Do you have creative areas you'd never want to do for money? What and why? Conversely, what creative areas do you wish you could monetize? What keeps you from "going pro" with those?
- The next time you freak out about not having enough time, remember what it felt like to be in a state of flow.

Did all your other responsibilities go away? Nope. But they did *to you* for that period. What does that tell you?
- For one week, track in 15-minute increments how you use your time. You will be stunned to learn what you spend your time on, and how much more time you might have to make something beautiful.
- The best way to discover your optimal rhythm (which can change over time or in different contexts) is through experimenting. If you prefer a fixed routine, try a week of mixing that up. If you're more flexible, see what happens when you work at the same time each day for a week. You'll never know if the alternatives work for you unless you try them.

RE-CREATION: *WRITING*

I have not always loved writing. Until my early 30s, I considered writing something you did to communicate your ideas. Nothing more. I appreciated great writing. I strove to make my own as adept as possible. My work required it. But I felt no deep pleasure in it. When I thought of friends who were writers, I wondered how they could spend all day just putting words on paper. It seemed boring to do nothing but write.

Over time, however, that changed. I can't remember the famous author who said this, but now I appreciate the sentiment. When an aspiring writer asked the veteran what it took to be a great novelist, the latter replied, "How do you feel about sentences?"

At some point, two things occurred for me. First, I learned to love sentences. I'm still not at the point of having a crush on individual words. I have some favorites such as "quench" or "lagoon." But I don't yet take a word as many a poet does and savor it, rolling it around my mouth like a lozenge. But at least now I understand why one would, and my esteem for and pleasure in poetry grows by the day.

Second, I discovered—far later than I should have—that writing is re-writing. Maybe one reason I didn't love writing was that it was so slow. It took me so long because I sought to craft the perfect work in the first draft. I'd noodle on each sentence rather than just getting something on paper and revising it later. Nothing has improved my writing so much as the freedom of bad first drafts and discovering the exquisite pleasure of Re-creation.

I doubt I will ever be a brilliant writer. But I hope to—I want to—be a better one. And I know that is possible if I continue to grow my love of sentences and seek to make better ones. Over and over. As with most creative practices, as they say, you learn to write by writing.

CHAPTER 9
RE-CREATION

Where you get started in a new field by re-creating the work of others and you improve your own work through refinement, renewal, and resurrection.

The patterns are simple, but followed together, they make for a whole that is wiser than the sum of its parts. Go for a walk; cultivate hunches; write everything down, but keep your folders messy; embrace serendipity; make generative mistakes; take on multiple hobbies; frequent coffeehouses and other liquid networks; follow the links; let others build on your ideas; borrow, recycle; reinvent. Build a tangled bank.
— Steven Johnson

Your first draft is a petulant teenager, sure it knows best, adamant that its Mother is wrong. Your third draft has emerged from puberty, realising that its Mother was right about everything.
— Angeline Trevena

Writing without revising is the literary equivalent of waltzing gaily out of the house in your underwear.
— Patricia Fuller

All good writing is rewriting. Most making of beauty is refining the ordinary into something exquisite. Without Re-creation of you, you never grow or *become* the person capable of making something good, true, and beautiful. Without

Re-creation of your work, it never achieves its full potential. You and your work develop through the hard and committed practice of re-work. It is the most effective way to learn and build mastery, the best way to hone your tastes and instincts, and the surest way to find out what resonates with your audience.

Plus, Re-creation is one hyphen away from "recreation," which sounds like fun. I find that an encouraging reminder when I'm slogging through all the revisions that are needed to transform the ugly mess of a first draft into something wonderful.

Only God creates something out of nothing. For the rest of us, we're all futzing about in various stages of re-creating. The writer of Ecclesiastes had it right about what's new under the sun. Even the most seemingly original work builds on what has come before.

Re-creation is about making things better—our work, us, others, and our world. No great creative product starts complete (though I have seen some newborns that strangely resemble old men). We, and our work, are in a constant state of refinement, even redemption.

My friend Brian, a pastor, once preached about how redemption (or restoration) is better than creation. I didn't buy it at first. But he pointed out how, for example, you're more overjoyed when you find your favorite pen that you'd lost than when you first received it. Or why the shepherd leaves the ninety-nine for the one. Or the rejoicing over the returned prodigal son, a day likely more celebratory than the son's birthday.

Re-creation is like Kit Kat bars in Japan: it comes in more varieties than you ever expected. It includes reinventing yourself in a new career, repurposing your work in a new medium or channel, or re-creating a feeling so that others experience the same emotion. Or it may be as simple as re-reading your notes from a book—then reconstructing them to understand how it all fits together. In this sense, even reflection can be a form of Re-creation.

Of all the ways to understand Re-creation, I'll focus here on those I've found to be the most helpful in creating adventurously.

RE-CREATION AS APPRENTICESHIP

Let's start with using Re-creation to learn in a new creative area. One of the best ways to make progress in a field is by having a mentor. With Re-creation, you can have many. Here, you glean elements from each by copying aspects of their work. Not to plagiarize, but to learn their techniques and thinking.

Mentors, whether one or many, in-person or online, rarely come to you. You must find them and ask them. If you think that takes too much effort, just look at the example of Johann Sebastian Bach.

In 1705, at age twenty, Bach was then the organist at a church in Arnstadt. He apparently (the details of this whole narrative are murky) requested leave for four weeks from his position.

He was gone for four months.

During that time, he walked 280 miles in winter to Lubeck to hear and potentially be mentored by Dieterich Buxtehude, then the greatest composer for the organ in the world. We don't know the details of what happened during Bach's time with Buxtehude. But we do know this: Bach's music after his visit was different. Initially, the people hated it. It was too unusual, too dramatic. And yet, the genius of Bach we know today was formed by the Re-creation of Buxtehude's work and his influence on Bach's style.[31]

A more contemporary version of how re-creating the work of others can move us forward comes from musician and author Andrew Peterson who notes in *Adorning the Dark,* "If you're stuck, pick your favorite songwriter and try writing a song like her. Imagine you're writing it for her to sing. Use her tricks, her grooves, her structures. In the end, you'll have something that's reminiscent of her, but is still yours."[32]

RE-CREATING FROM MANY SOURCES

To keep you from mimicking just one creator, it helps to broaden your range of sources. In *Steal Like an Artist,* Austin Kleon notes:

> …*you don't just steal from one of your heroes, you steal from all of them. The writer Wilson Mizner said if you copy from one author, it's plagiarism, but if you copy from many, it's research. I once heard the cartoonist Gary Panter say, 'If you have one person you're influenced by, everyone will say you're the next whoever. But if you rip off a hundred people, everyone will say you're so original!' What to copy is a little bit trickier. Don't just steal the style, steal the thinking behind the style. You don't want to look like your heroes, you want to see like your heroes.*[33]

This isn't a new thought. Learning from those that have gone before us is as old as art itself. As Goethe put it around 200 years ago, "He who cannot draw on three thousand years is living from hand to mouth."[34] And one element that can be most helpful to "steal" from others is learning their technique.

THE VALUE OF TECHNIQUE

To me, skill is your general ability to do something. Technique is a specific method. You can build your skill in painting through practice, but you can speed up your ability to paint leaves, for example, by learning the technique of pressing down on the side of your brush. I used to think of technique as akin to tying your shoes—something needed, but not overly exciting. Now I see technique like the old FastPass at Disney World. It gets you to the good places quicker. Let me give you an example from the world of drawing.

With representational drawing, you must learn to see and then record what is there, not your idealized or symbolized view of it. At least that's what they teach you. And part of it is true. You want your drawings to look like what is there. But here's the dirty secret it took me years to learn: It's all an illusion. You don't really draw what you see. You translate a three-dimensional subject into a two-dimensional medium so that your audience sees what you want them to see. Therein lies the creativity. You're not a camera. You must make adjustments on paper to record what is before you so that the drawing *reads* well to your audience.

To do so, you must learn to see so you can perceive distances, proportions, angles, etc. But the way you make the drawing look right is often more technique gained through Re-creation than talent. Try this exercise to see what I mean.

Draw a house on the hill like this:

At this stage, you're re-creating a scene you likely did in elementary school. Now comes the illusion. Add a few more hills:

Add walls and a roof as seen from an angle. This simple trick or technique just increased the sense of dimensionality.

Now, add shading—maybe even a pathway to the door:

Voila! Compare it to the Step One house. It looks pretty good, doesn't it? You increased the verisimilitude, not by increasing your talent or even your ability to see. What improved the drawing was all technique, the little tricks of adding perspective and shading.

Technique alone will never be enough to make great creative work, since on its own it can be lifeless. But the more you work on improving your techniques, the faster you get to mastery. Best of all, technique allows you to repeat what works in different projects rather than just hoping lightning will strike twice.

QUANTITY LEADS TO QUALITY

The way to internalize technique is through repetition, re-creating the same kind of work over and over. An oft-repeated story captures this well:

The ceramics teacher announced on opening day that he was dividing the class into two groups. All those on the left side of the studio, he said, would be graded solely on the quantity of work they produced, all those on the right solely on its quality. His procedure was simple: on the final day of class he would bring in his bathroom scales and weigh the work of the 'quantity' group: fifty pounds of pots rated an 'A', forty pounds a 'B', and so on. Those being graded on 'quality', however, needed to produce only one pot — albeit a perfect one — to get an 'A'. Well, came grading time and a curious fact emerged: the works of highest quality were all produced by the group being graded for quantity. It seems that while the 'quantity' group was busily churning out piles of work and learning from their mistakes — the 'quality' group had sat theorizing about perfection, and in the end had little more to show for their efforts than grandiose theories and a pile of dead clay.[35]

This idea of quantity leading to quality occurs on two levels. In the ceramics example, Re-creation occurs over multiple different pieces, increasing both your ability and your own sense of what quality looks and feels like gained through experimenting and experience. Within a single work, say, writing a novel, the quantity of drafts and edits leads to the refinement of that work. You could say that with edits, you're improving the object. With repetitive practice, you're improving you. You need both forms of Re-creation to gain mastery.

MAKE/DO TO KNOW

Flannery O'Connor once quipped, "I write because I don't know what I think until I read what I say." And that can involve not just your initial words, but those refined through Re-creation. Re-creation helps us process and reflect. But it can also uncover ideas that weren't even there when you started.

In the Renaissance, Michelangelo and Leonardo Da Vinci transformed how we think about creativity. Not just because of their remarkable skills, but because of their approach to Re-creation. In 15th century Italy, artists and scholars believed that creativity, or *invenzione* as they phrased it, occurred in the imagination. You had an idea in your mind, and you manifested it through your art or craft. What the existent drawings of Michelangelo and Leonardo reveal, however, is that those two often worked in reverse. A drawing might express a concept, but then it might lead to a brand-new idea. We think of ideation as king and making as the second step. But this shows that it is often the making that leads to more or clearer ideas.

Many of Michelangelo's designs for architectural projects, such as the design of St. Peter's Church in Rome, started out as drawings of human figures. In the noodling and restating of lines on the drawings of people, new possibilities for architectural elements emerged. This human figure transformed into that column, etc. Thus, with Re-creation, you both ideate to make and make to ideate.[36]

PURSUING A CONCEPT OVER TIME

Re-creation can also mean repeating your own work multiple times, both to gain mastery and also to get to know it better. The sculptor Constantin Brâncuși did multiple versions of his Bird in Space sculpture. Artist Chuck Close painted his self-portrait in different ways over decades. Neither just made copies of past works or did production runs. Instead, they re-created their pieces into something new. Each version informed the next.

In this sense, Re-creation is about finding what fascinates you and then pursuing it in as much depth as you need. Each Re-creation gets you closer to the heart or essence of the thing. Thus, you may find that the entire purpose of version one was to get you to version five.

REDIRECTION AND RESURRECTION

When you're taking risks, big or small, you'll have some missteps. When that happens and the work veers off course, you have several forms of Re-creation in your toolkit. You can re-do it, repair it, or repurpose it. With the latter, you take certain elements and apply them to an additional work, perhaps even in a different medium, such as using lyrics from a song that didn't come together as the basis for a screenplay. But two of my favorite forms of Re-creation are redirection and resurrection.

Instead of trying to repair the work so it appears as planned, a redirection (or "design reconsideration") means you alter the plan. It's a silver-linings way of rethinking what the end product could be. The results are often better than the initial intent. This ties to trusting God with the outcomes, even if at the moment it may feel like a failure. Remember: until the ultimate step, you never know how the story will end. Which is why, as Robert Cormier points out for authors, "The beautiful part of writing is that you don't have to get it right the first time, unlike, say, a brain surgeon."[37]

My favorite form of Re-creation, however, is the resurrection. This shows up in two ways. First is a created work that outlasts its original intent, as in architecture and old buildings. As Roger Scruton notes in *Beauty*, the buildings built around function-only tend to get demolished. But those built with some aesthetic intent get repurposed. Look at old, yet beautiful brick warehouses now used for expensive boutiques or lofts. Beauty lends itself to Re-creation because we recognize something of value there that we want to preserve—even resurrect.

The second form of resurrection is more personal. It's where you give up on a work but later, you revisit it and realize that something vital still lies within. Thus, you take a dead project and give it a new life. I just finished a side table. I had made the base thirty years ago but put it aside. It had water stains from sitting in the garage and seemed destined for the scrap pile. But I resurrected it, planing off the water damage, sanding out the scratches, and designing a new top. This side table looks nothing like the original. It is much better. And now, I'm more enamored with this piece than anything I could have made from new wood. We do, indeed, value more what was lost but is now found.

MAKING RE-CREATION EASIER

By now, you're probably realizing how vast Re-creation is. It can show up as apprenticeship or the mastering of a technique. It can require multiple iterations or a single one that reveals a new idea. It may mean exploring a concept over and over or refining one through redirection or even resurrection. All of this can seem daunting. But it doesn't have to be if you remember that Re-creation is like a safety net and a new form of exploration all in one. It is both the art of second chances—of grace—and the surest path to better.

QUESTIONS AND EXPLORATIONS

- Sometimes it helps, when learning from the works of others, to isolate the variables. For example, instead of attempting to just copy a Degas pastel scene of dancers, focus on one element at a time: lighting, strokes, colors, poses, angles, etc. You'll not only learn more, but you'll also get less overwhelmed. What is one aspect of your creative work that you want to focus on right now to re-create?
- Who and what have you re-created in the past? What did you learn? It helps to think about the learning. Just copying because you like a style is fine. But when you get clear on what you like and what you're gleaning, you can more readily apply those lessons to other projects.
- What are specific techniques you could practice in your medium? Even advanced creators can always learn new techniques. The key is finding those that seem interesting to you or that can shore up weak areas. For painters, that might mean learning to use thumbnails of tonal sketches to improve contrast. Or for novelists, learning to improve point of view (POV). What are three new techniques you'd like to learn?

DISCOVERY: *TRAVEL*

In *Hidden Travel*, I quote former *Los Angeles Times* travel editor Catharine Hamm who told me that travel is creative because travel involves problem solving. And solving problems lies at the heart of creativity. But not everyone agrees with this perspective.

I have friends who travel who don't see themselves as creative in the least. I have artist friends who don't see travel or even problem solving as creative. I understand each perspective. But here's where I differ.

Creativity shows up in many guises. As we saw earlier, one helpful differentiation is between compositional and improvisational creativity. Writing a book, song, sonnet, or score is compositional. That's how most people think of creativity. But improvisational creativity, the ability to make things up on the fly, can be as powerful and is probably practiced more widely. Jazz musicians and improv comedians come to mind. But so too do busy moms juggling competing demands, athletes determining their next move, and travelers navigating a foreign culture. Any form of problem solving for which there is no known "right" answer can be creative.

Travel has helped me build my improvisational creativity skills. In turn, those have improved my ability to discover. I see more because I don't settle for the obvious choices. On a trip, that means going to less-visited locations or pursuing local options not usually pursued by tourists. I'm willing to take greater risks—and discover new things—because I know I can back my way out of most situations. As my problem-solving skills have grown, so too has my ingenuity and confidence to handle new situations without the angst I once had for the unfamiliar.

In traveling to over 50 countries and in all my creative efforts, what I've most discovered is God's faithfulness. The farther I go, the closer we get. And the more I realize just how much discovery itself—seeing the things I am meant to see—is a gift.

CHAPTER 10
DISCOVERY

Where you see things differently by using all your senses (including spiritual ones) to collect, connect, and share.

To every age Christ dies anew and is resurrected within the imagination of man... If every Bible is lost, if every church crumbles to dust, if the last believer in the last prayer opens her eyes and lets it all finally go, Christ will appear on this earth as calmly and casually as he appeared to the disciples walking to Emmaus after his death, who did not recognize this man to whom they had pledged their very lives; this man whom they had seen beaten, crucified, abandoned by God; this man who, after walking the dusty road with them, after sharing an ordinary meal and discussing the scriptures, had to vanish once more in order to make them see.

— Christian Wiman, *My Bright Abyss*

They are ill discoverers that think there is no land when they can see nothing but sea.
— Francis Bacon

Discovery is more than finding something new to you. It is about new ways of perceiving the world: making connections that others don't, seeing what others miss, caring about details that others deem irrelevant. You can't create adventurously without discovery.

In Amanda Palmer's book, *The Art of Asking*, she offers yet another way of defining the creative process as three stages:

Collect, Connect, and Share. With Collect, you gather up ideas, raw materials, and sparks of inspiration. In Connect, you assemble those into an innovative product, service, or experience. You then Share that with the world. I like the simplicity of this version and how each stage carries with it a form of discovery: in the world, in your own processing, and through relationships with others.

That discovery, however, rarely happens without intentionality on our part. As author Robertson Davies puts it, "The eye sees only what the mind is prepared to comprehend." We do not see if we are not looking. And even then, what we see with our eyes isn't all that is there.

DISCOVERING THROUGH A GOD HUNT

When our two sons were little, we practiced God Hunts. They are intentional efforts to see God all around you. The key here is to give God the benefit of the doubt. You assume God is part of all that you behold. When we started, usually on a drive somewhere, one son might point out two perpendicular branches on a tree and say, "Oh, there's one! It's a cross!" Over time, they became more discerning, but still maintained a sense of wonder at all the ways God can appear in the world.

I learned several things from these God Hunts. First, they are harder to do than you think. Like abiding with Jesus, it sounds easy until you practice it and find out just how prone we are to distraction. Second, they've made me aware of how little I see each day. Finally, I realized how much I take God for granted. What I write off as coincidence most of the time becomes, on a God Hunt, an explicit recognition of minor miracles or answers to prayer.

You can apply this God Hunt to any phase of the creative process. When you do, you see unlikely connections and experience a greater sense of wondrous gratitude. In looking back at the end of a project—even on something as seemingly unartistic as a departmental reorganization— and I see all the details and "coincidences" that came together, I cannot take credit for the results. Few things lead me to worship as surely as recognizing how God has showed up and made the whole thing possible.

PAYING ATTENTION IN LOVE

A similar approach to a God Hunt is an exercise known as Paying Attention in Love. This one helps you employ all your senses to discover. Here's what I wrote in *Hidden Travel* about this practice:

(This exercise) derives from a practice in the book Awaken Your Senses *by J. Brent Bill and Beth A. Booram. Here's how it works:*

Find a place where you can concentrate for five to ten minutes. Sit comfortably and list three things that you see, hear, smell, taste (if possible), and touch (or feel, like the seat beneath you). Basically, you're doing an exercise in mindfulness and noticing with all of your senses.

Now do the exercise again. Three of each: seeing, hearing, smelling, tasting and feeling. Maybe these are the same objects, maybe new ones. But here's the difference: This time, don't just pay attention. Pay attention in love. By this I mean notice each object or sensation and attribute a positive association or meaning to it. See it through the eyes of a lover looking upon her beloved. Listen from a perspective of gratitude. Smell as if you're valuing the scent highly. Touch as if feeling for the first time.

I first tried this exercise at home. On the initial round, I noticed my guitar propped up in a corner. 'There's my guitar,' I thought. But on the second round, when I saw that same instrument, by paying attention in love, I was filled with a deep gratitude for the gift of music and was reminded of the immense joy I get from playing. Same object, but viewed with the filter of appreciation, it changed not just what I saw, but how much I saw. It changed me.[38]

I do this exercise when I'm stuck, need re-centering, or desire inspiration. It's surprising how something so simple can reveal so much and can cultivate a deeper appreciation and even worship for all the ways God blesses me.

A similar approach comes from poet Maggie Smith in her book, *Keep Moving*. She explains how she has taught her children to be aware of "beauty emergencies" that she defines as "one of those things you have to look at now, before it's gone."[39] Examples include rainbows, sunsets, interesting birds and animals, certain lights and shadows, etc. These aren't practical moments. They are small and fleeting. Like small acts of love, they can pass unheeded or without recognition of their significance. Just like your creative work. It all comes down to paying attention and a*ppreciating* in love what you see.

GO NARROW

This form of careful attention can mean constant scanning for something new. But to keep from being overwhelmed, I practice something we've already covered: Focus on what's interesting to you. You already do this subconsciously when you skim a web page or magazine. But if you make an intentional decision to seek that which appeals to you, and—this is key—you ignore the rest, you'll make the process of discovery more fruitful and enjoyable. You keep your senses alert, but with intent. In doing so, I've found that what I *don't* discover can be as valuable as what I do. Just as white noise helps block out unwanted sounds, tuning out all the SQUIRREL!-inducing distractions makes the discovery process more rewarding and manageable.

Narrowing your focus can also include maintaining that focus longer. Author and Italy expert Fred Plotkin writes about narrowing focus when viewing art in Florence:

Like it or not, one must adopt a policy of 'Poco, ma buono' (loosely translated as 'Do less, but do it really well') to experi-

ence what Florence has to offer. A mad dash through a gallery will leave you with only fleeting impressions. Spend ten minutes in front of one painting and you will see remarkable things that a two-minute look could not reveal; spend an hour in front of that same painting and your life will be changed. To really pause and reflect, whether in front of a sculpture or a dish of gelato, is to find the presence of art and genius in all things.[40]

GO WIDE

Going narrow provides focus. But sometimes you'll want to expand what interests you to get out of a rut. One well-tested approach is to visit a library, bookstore, or newsstand and peruse magazines covering subjects new to you. That might mean diverse topics such as hot rods, opera, natural health remedies, chainsaw art, or weddings. You're not exploring these to cultivate new hobbies or expertise (though you never know). You're fueling your ability in divergent thinking by collecting insights beyond your current interests. You don't have to do this all the time. But periodic, intentional forays into new areas keep you and your creative thinking fresh. All of this is a form of exploration that, at the time, may not seem relevant. But as we're about to see, it may be the start of something big.

EXPLORE THEN EXPLOIT

Quiz time. What do you think is the primary commonality between creative people who have had extended "hot streaks," meaning they had significant periods of success in their field, whether art, science, or business? Is it their length of experience? Age? Education? Quantity of work produced? The time spent practicing? None of those. The researchers who examined the career work of over 20,000 artists, scientists, and film directors summarized the answer in just three words: "Explore, then exploit."

Economist Dashun Wang, who led the research, found that *artists and scientists tend to experiment with diverse styles or topics before their hot streak begins. This period of exploration is followed by a period of creatively productive focus. 'Our data shows that people ought to explore a bunch of things at work, deliberate about the best fit for their skills, and then exploit what they've learned,' Wang said. This precise sequence—exploration, followed by exploitation—was the single best predictor of the onset of a hot streak.*[41]

Wang uses the example of painter Jackson Pollock who experimented in a wide range of styles before landing on the drip paintings he did for four years in the late 1940s. They made him one of the world's most famous artists at the time, but soon after, he gave them up to explore new areas.

Such exploration works not only on the career level, but also for projects. Experimenting with different styles, tools, materials, and techniques is a form of discovery. You don't think your way into a solution. You experiment your way there, often using your body and spirit as much as your mind. The songwriter mixes up chord progressions, changes the bridge, or revises the melody to fit new lyrics. The entrepreneur tests her new company's offerings through multiple prototypes. The potter feels her way into a new way of folding over the lip of a vase. In any field, experimentation—which leads to discovery—is your way of exploring until you exploit.

The exploit phase involves specialization, but only after the previous period of wider exploration through diverse experiences. That exploration phase can feel like a waste of time since you *produce* so little. But without this seed-planting period of discovery, you won't harvest the productive streaks later in the exploit mode. You need both.

This brings us back to my limiting mindset that my creative efforts must have a clear, others-oriented purpose to be pleasing to God. Time in the explore mode, however, may produce nothing for others. And yet, it could be the secret to the later exploit phase which can. We can't know whether what seems like a waste today could be the foundation of tomorrow's breakthrough.

And so, in summary, we make. We discover. We explore. We exploit. And through it all, we abide with Jesus. We see what he'd have us see—with all our senses. We turn every day into a God Hunt, every project or even moment into an opportunity to pay attention in love. We focus on what interests us, but we also scan widely and strive to be open in every stage of the creative process.

Such efforts help us discover what and how *we* need to create. But there's another side to all this as well: helping others to discover.

HELPING OTHERS TO DISCOVER

Often, when I talk to creatives about helping others discover their work, they think I mean marketing or promotion. And that is part of it. But even if people *find* your work, what will they discover in it?

Novelist Aimee Bender points out for writers, "If you are not surprised or you are not discovering, the reader will probably find the work to be flat or predictable."[42] It's why, when I'm reading out loud something I've written and I find my mind wandering, I know the reader will do the same. I must discover what interests or better, surprises *me* with what I'm writing about. If not, the results won't sing for others.

Then, I need to consider ways to add depth to my work. Almost all powerful, lasting creative work has layers, much like an onion or Shrek. In cooking, we talk about layers of flavor. In painting, you often get a richer image through multiple thin washes of paint or glazes. A *good* book has a compelling plot, interesting characters, and dramatic conflict. A *great* book has all of those plus a deeper theme or moral. The more we build layers of meaning into our work, the more there is for others to discover.

Our audiences, however, must be ready to discover our work. You can expose them to it through ads, social media, gallery appearances, etc. But you can only push this so far. A person not interested in science fiction may see dozens of ads for your battle droid novel, but those won't register. Or, even if they like sci-fi, they may not be looking for your version of it. You can expose people to your work. But you can't force them to like it.

I learned a great deal about this during our own time in Florence, Italy. In a congested, touristy city, my wife and I found a quiet oasis one day at the 13th-century Church of Ognissanti. When we entered early that morning, the church was empty except for two nuns and one other visitor. Lovely choral music played in the background as we marveled at the works of Giotto, Ghirlandaio, and Botticelli (who is buried there).

We spoke with one of the nuns, Sister Laura. My wife and I shared with her our awe of the holiness and beauty in that place. We asked if most people felt that there. She said that we *saw* the beauty there because we *understood* the beauty there. We explained how, before this trip, we had studied up on works of the Renaissance so that now we understood at least a little about these famous artists. She noted that most people walk in and only see "paintings."

When I asked if it frustrated her that others don't appreciate all that is there, she said no. That God works in each person to touch them at the right time and way. Some do respond to the beauty and holiness of that church. To her, that is enough. It is not her role to convince them, just to be available to the curious and to share appropriately when asked.

It reminded me of a line from Tyler Staton, "Prayer cannot be taught. It can only be discovered."[43] So it is with the things that move us most. I can't convince you to like, much less love, my new favorite song, painting, poem, or anything. You must discover your own way into it. When you're ready.

And yet, as creators, we can help in that. We can make experiences of delight around our creative work to increase the likelihood of it being discovered and valued. People do judge books by their covers. They pay attention to how a painting is framed. The comfort of a theater's seat affects one's feelings about the play. Thus, we can be conscious of, and seek to optimize the ancillary factors that encourage and inspire discovery. From first exposure, say, in an ad or our storefront display, to behind-the-scenes videos, to the testimonials of customers and fans, we can think beyond the creative work itself to the overall experience a person has in engaging in that work. The more we help them, the greater the likelihood of them discovering and appreciating what we make.

There are layers of discovery, just as there are layers of meaning in much of the work you create. And when you can help others experience the depths of those, you realize why you're doing this crazy work of making. And why helping others to discover can be one of the most powerful and rewarding experiences of your life. Not just of your work. But parts of you. And glimpses into the Creator who shines through it all and leads us in paths of endless discovery.

QUESTIONS AND EXPLORATIONS

- The Shakers finished the undersides of tables and the backs of drawers, places few people look. Why? Because they believed that "God sees everything." How do you react to that level of attention to detail and finishing? What details could you add to a current project that would make it richer or help people discover something powerful?
- Never underestimate the power of exploration. As the authors of *Wired to Create* note, "Together, these findings suggest that the drive for exploration, in its many forms, may be the single most important personal factor predicting creative achievement."[44] What does exploration

look like in your own creative process? How could it relate to a current project?
- Find three things within a block of your home that you've never noticed before. Jot those down in a notebook. Do the same thing every day for a week. Do you see any patterns? Any creative sparks from any of these?

MOVEMENT: *FLY FISHING*

How is fly fishing creative? One of my sons once made a brilliant observation about what constitutes creativity: "If it involves a creative decision, it's creative." Following a recipe isn't creative. There's no creative decision there. But making a delicious meal from the five ingredients in your fridge is creative since it requires creative decisions.

You see where this is going. With fly fishing, you must make several creative decisions: where to go, where to cast your fly, what fly to use, what line to use, how to present the fly, how long (on a river) to let it drift, how to match your artificial fly to the insects in the water and air around you.

I love fishing on rivers because of the movement: of the water, of your fly in the water, of proceeding up or downstream, and most of all, the casting. There's a progression with learning to cast a fly line. You start confused, looking more like a lion tamer with a whip. Then, you get to a level of proficiency where you can form this virtual Aurora Borealis of fly line behind you on your backcast, a whirling symphony of filament that looks straight out of *A River Runs Through It*.

Eventually, you reach a point where you appreciate the wisdom of the old guys who tell you, "A fly in the air catches no fish." And you get your casts down to precise motions. It's still all about movement, but more efficient and controlled.

Most of all, fly fishing is, to me, a metaphor for creativity. You practice. You learn all you can. You master your tools. But there's still no guarantee you'll catch anything.

Here's the key: It doesn't matter. Sure, landing a fish is great. But to me, fly fishing, like creating, can be worship. On a river 20 minutes from my home, I can stand midstream at dusk, watching the bald eagle soar overhead as a family of beavers comes into view on one bank, and a deer emerges on the other. I'm doing something creative I love in a place I love with the One I most love. Catching a fish is just a bonus.

CHAPTER 11
MOVEMENT

Where you avoid stuckness, keep going at any stage of the creative process, and maintain momentum in all your creative work.

You don't drown by falling in the water. You drown by staying there.
— Edwin Louis Cole

It had long since come to my attention that people of accomplishment rarely sat back and let things happen to them. They went out and happened to things.
— Elinor Smith, *Aviatrix*

Be impatient for action but patient for outcomes.
— Dan Heath, *Upstream: The Quest to Solve Problems Before They Happen*

Movement, that sense of forward motion and progress, is essential to creating adventurously. No one I know enjoys feeling stuck. But how you keep moving isn't always intuitive.

Personally, I find one of the hardest things about creativity—or movement in The Creative Wild—is that we believe it shouldn't be so hard. But if it weren't hard, everyone would create more than they do (which would be good). And it wouldn't be as rewarding (which would be bad).

One of the most liberating moments in my creative journey was the day I read this line from Elizabeth Gilbert's book, *Big Magic*: "Frustration is not an interruption of your process; frustration is the process." Could that really be true? That frustration isn't something to fight or avoid, but something to, dare I say it, embrace?

Yes. Here's what I've learned.

Frustration is the norm. It won't go away. It shouldn't go away—for reasons we're about to explore. But its ability to depress or diminish you should. Creativity is struggle. You're giving birth to something new. Women delivering babies—an extreme example of creating—don't do their nails and talk about the fun they're having. You work through the incompletion, the unknowing, the false starts, the "I can'ts" and the head-banging-what-do-I-do-now's. Not because they are enjoyable. But because they are the process. And you—yes, you—have something the 99% of people who never try lack: The courage and drive to move through the frustration and the ambiguity. Until POP! Something comes together (or a baby emerges). And it all makes sense. And the way forward is both clear and screaming at you to get a move on. And you do. You keep moving. Even if it is hard. No, make that *because* it is hard.

IT ISN'T MAGIC

The difficulty of creating can seem like a downer. But it is just the opposite: you and I know how to do hard work. There's no special ability or secret formula needed. As Kevin Ashton puts it in *How to Fly a Horse*:

> *If we want to create, we must, in the words of Paul Gallico, open our veins and bleed. There are no secrets. When we ask writers about their process or scientists about their methods or inventors where they get their ideas from, we are hoping for something that doesn't exist: a trick, recipe, or ritual to summon the magic—an alternative to work. There isn't one. To create is to work. It is that easy and that hard.*[45]

Realizing creating is hard work removes the scaffolding behind this blind hope (and fear) that there's a miracle solution. We don't have to be extraordinary or talented or genius. We only need to know how to work. And then do it.

Too often, I get stuck simply because I resist doing what I know I can and should do. I want immediate gratification, not the almost physical pain of having to wrestle with ideas that either overwhelm or desert me. I want flow and that dizzy sense of inspiration and excitement all the time, like a continual caffeine buzz. But it doesn't come or stay continuously any more than those spiritual highs when we sense God's presence.

When I pursue the feeling of flow over the hard work of creating, I'm chasing the wrong goal. And when nothing happens, it's easy to classify the frustration as a heightened form of being stuck, a creative block akin to the oft-repeated concept of writer's block.

Ashton, however, reminds us of this:

The condition is not writer's block, it is write-something-I-think-is-good block. The cure is self-evident: write something you think is bad. Writer's block is the mistake of believing in constant peak performance. Peaks cannot be constant; they are, by definition, exceptional. You will have good days and less good days, but the only bad work you can do is the work you do not do. Great creators work whether they feel like it or not, whether they are in the mood or not, whether they are inspired or not. Be chronic, not acute. Success doesn't strike; it accumulates.[46]

My friend, the writer Matt Mikalatos, felt he had writer's block during a creative writing course in college. He told his writing professor about it. The professor told him to come back with a 30-page paper by that time the next day. It could be on any topic, but it had to be 30 pages. Matt turned in the hard-to-pull-off paper on time. "Still have writer's block?" asked the professor. "No," replied Matt. Then or ever since.

The way forward—the secret of movement—is movement. Even if what you're making seems like garbage, you're still making. Why is the almost universal solution to starting anything this: make a really stinking bad first draft? Because out of that comes the good stuff. There are multiple techniques (you'll find more at www.ExploreYourWorlds.com/movement) for getting unstuck creatively. But if you look at the ones that work the best, most involve inherent movement:

- Take a walk or exercise (probably the all-time most effective way to get unstuck)
- Change your environment or perspective
- Pivot to another creative project
- Work on a different aspect of this project
- Make marks (meaning, just get something down without a purpose, such as doodle, write your Morning Pages, cut up and remix collage materials, paint blobs, practice chord progressions, etc.)
- Set limits (which, as we'll see in the chapter on Incompletion, may seem the opposite of movement but can enhance it). These could be time limits, word counts for writers, size limits for painters (e.g., do a 2" x 3" painting), etc.
- Talk to others or collaborate
- Get outside yourself. Imagine a friend in your circumstance. What advice would you give them?
- Intentionally disrupt your rhythms by attempting to do the opposite of your normal approach or routine
- Get going on that terrible first draft

The best advice on getting unstuck? Don't get stuck to begin with. Create the structures and systems—the routines or practices—that help you show up and work, even if you're not feeling motivated. Work at the same time of day or same place, organize your tools and materials well so you don't have to think about where to find things (and thus have an excuse not to), end each day with the next step all ready for the following day, etc.

Best of all, combine these forms of structure with the notion of energy modes we explored in Chapter 8 on Rhythm. Those have been a game changer for me. Structure and routines or practices get me to the place where I don't rely on emotions to work. After all, as Paul Raymond Martin notes, "Nowhere in a book contract does it say, 'If you feel like it.'"[47] But when your systems or routines falter (as even the best practices will at times), paradoxically, I switch back to what I feel like doing to break through. This combination of structure/routines and energy modes is a powerful way to not only foster movement but to build momentum.

Momentum is challenging to start, but once you get it going, it is hard to stop. And it's all based on this idea that movement begets movement. It's only when we think that movement will be easy that it isn't.

MOVEMENT NEEDS FRICTION

What makes movement, in the physical sense, hard is that as you get going, friction builds up. The faster that space capsule hurtles toward earth on re-entry, the hotter it gets. But that same friction can be essential to your progress. You can't make your way forward on icy roads without friction or traction.

"It's not an adventure until something goes wrong." This line from Patagonia founder Yvon Chouinard reflects an uncomfortable truth about creating adventurously. We may not want friction—setbacks, suffering, discomfort of any kind—and yet, we need it to give us the traction required for our best work and sense of adventure. We need something to challenge us, something we can press against and struggle with. We try to avoid suffering and yet, it is during the hardest periods of our lives that we most grow.

Without the friction of discomfort, we go on autopilot in our relationship with God and even our creativity. Sure, we want flow. But flow only happens when we're working on something hard, something inherently filled with friction. Otherwise, we slip over the smooth surfaces or just spin.

We see friction as nothing but an impediment because we see productivity as king. But movement in The Creative Wild is more jungle trek than superhighway dash. It's why prototyping and iteration almost always outperforms the "next big thing" plunge. Movement through experimentation and re-creations, because of the inherent friction, allows you to consider more and better possibilities. It's also why, sometimes, the best way to get moving is to rest. I can't count the times I tried to push through something in the evening and got nowhere only to find that not only does "joy come with the morning" (Psalm 30:5), but very often, so does the creative breakthrough.

Friction shows up in all stages of our creative work. But a surprising example happens in the ideation phase. Most people think all their great ideas occur at the start or early in a brainstorming session when they are fresh. When those ideas and their energy run out, they figure they are done. Anything after that will be the dregs. Not so. Research shows that when most people think they've exhausted all their ideas, when they encounter friction and think they should stop, that's when they're tapping into the best ones.[48]

THE WONDER OF THE NEXT STEP

Sometimes, we do run out of steam, fresh ideas, or momentum and we need to turn around and start over. But that's an extreme measure and useful primarily when you feel hopelessly lost rather than just stuck. A more common solution is to keep moving, but to shorten your stride, so to speak. This involves narrowing your focus from the big picture to the next step.

This concept of the next step, or baby steps, is so seemingly obvious and yet so under-practiced that it can be magical. It means you focus on the next step, not the next ten, or the next 100. You don't fret about what isn't done. Instead, you anticipate what can be. You're not deciding who to thank at the awards ceremony. You're figuring out how do I get through this next page. Or maybe the next sentence. Or next word.

Tiny next steps are particularly helpful in the messy middle stages of a project. At the outset, you're excited by the possibilities. Near the end, you see the finish line and speed up. But in the middle (the Valley of Despair as we'll see in Chapter 16, Incompletion), the secret to forward movement often lies in reducing the big picture down to baby steps or micro goals. This next-steps approach makes each phase more manageable, provides ongoing milestones and accomplishment, and reduces the likelihood of getting overwhelmed.

As in hiking, progress in The Creative Wild is this rhythm of "look down, look up." When the trail is rocky or filled with obstacles, I look down. When it is smoother, I look up and take in the scenery and maybe even where the trail leads. I need both perspectives. But I'll stumble and fall if I only look up, and I'll miss the reason for being out there if I only look down. And no matter what, when I arrive at my destination, it will rarely appear exactly as I imagined.

DOSES AND DIVES

Let's take this a step (pun intended) further. What stalls me a great deal is when I step away from a big project, say, writing a book, for some time. Then, I must reorient myself to it when I re-engage. There's a lot of lost momentum in that. But if I never get too far from it, I maintain that momentum. David Kadavy (who we met back in the chapter on Rhythms) has a concept called Minimum Creative Doses. Even a few minutes touching on one aspect of a project per day keeps it top of mind and active. I liken these doses to my favorite approach for learning, i.e., practicing for just fifteen minutes each day. You can find five to fifteen minutes in any day, particularly in those "wasted" slots between meetings or other activities, to do one thing on your project. Not necessarily a big thing or even a productive thing. Just something to keep you engaged with the project.

The key, I've found, is to keep a list, even a mental one, of all the small things I could do: write a few sentences, research sources, mix new colors, refine an outline, review a previous draft, etc. If I must spend five minutes just to think about how to spend those five minutes, I just lost those five minutes. But having a written or mental list of small next steps and then doing even one of them each day helps in so many ways. I'm more productive, I feel greater progress, and I'm encouraging incubation, since my subconscious brain has more to chew on. Most of all, I maintain and even build momentum.

I've found the five-to-fifteen-minute window effective. But Kadavy recommends only a few minutes:

Jot down just a few things, make a sketch, or hum a few bars into a recorder. Set a timer for two minutes if it helps. Then, forget about it. Go about whatever you were doing. Now, set a reminder. Remind yourself to revisit this idea the next day. Work on it again, just for a few minutes. It will be easier to make progress than it was the day before.[49]

Try a few different timeframes to see what length works best for you. Most of all, do these daily to get the greatest value from them.

For bigger projects, you'll also need the opposite of small doses, what I call deep dives. Cal Newport's book, *Deep Work*, has many pointers on how to maintain a deep focus on creative work. I particularly like his idea of shifting your thinking from carving out pockets in a distracted week for deep dives and focused work, to seeing your week as being all about deep dives. Then, from those deep dives, you create specific windows for less focused work like meetings, emails, social media, etc. His point is that distraction will always win out unless we contain it. Make the deep work your primary orientation and only do the distracting things in certain blocks, say, an hour for email once every four hours.

THE ROLE OF ACCEPTANCE

Whether small doses or deep dives, the key to movement through The Creative Wild is a form of acceptance. When I accepted—and even appreciated—that speed bumps and stumbling blocks, stuck moments and setbacks, disappointments and detours, that these actually aid moving forward, I experienced a remarkable sense of freedom. I'd been swimming against the riptide, trying to reach shore by heading toward it, thinking movement always meant a direct path. But when I embraced the challenges as key to better creative work, it was like swimming parallel to shore and then heading in. Recognizing and embracing the difficulty made it less of one.

Have I learned to like suffering and setbacks? Nope. But now, I keep them in perspective. I remember what Jesus said: "I have told you these things, so that in me you may have peace. In this world, you will have trouble. But take heart! I have overcome the world." (John 16:33). And so I do. I don't obsess about the trouble part. Instead, I take heart.

And then I keep moving.

QUESTIONS AND EXPLORATIONS

- Does this notion that creating is simply hard work, and that movement requires friction, encourage or discourage you? Why? Think of the most rewarding creative project you've ever done. Then ask how much of it was easy and how much was hard. It's a good reminder that hard can be good.

- In Todd Henry's book, *The Accidental Creative,* he recommends carrying a 3" x 5" card with you everywhere. On it, you write three big ideas you're wrestling with. Take it further. On the other side, write down three things you could do in fifteen minutes or less. You'll likely be scratching these out and replacing them often, but maintaining the list maintains the momentum.
- Heed this advice from author Anne Lamott: "The best thing you can do to write your book is to stop not doing it. Just stop it." And the best way to stop not doing it is to break it down to baby steps. What are three baby steps you could take on that new creative project right now?

PERSPECTIVE: *SKETCHING*

I took the first and last drawing class in my life about three decades ago. I remember the almost physical pain of not being able to reproduce in my drawing the image before me. After that, I barely tried to draw for ten years.

I wish I knew then what I know now. If I had just approached drawing from a different perspective, I'd have so much more experience in doing it by now. But all things in God's timing.

Three people have helped me most in learning not just to draw, but to overcome the belief that I cannot do so. The first was one of my sons, who, before college, couldn't draw much better than I could. After one semester of art classes, he was making some remarkable drawings. What made the difference? Practice and perspective.

Not just linear perspective, the scientific understanding of how to represent a three-dimensional object on paper. But the perspective that yes, I can do this. Initially for him, and then later for me.

The other two sources of help have been authors, Danny Gregory and David Koeder. With Gregory and his books such as *The Creative License: Giving Yourself Permission to Be the Artist You Truly Are* and others, I found someone who just drew, without worrying whether the drawings were perfect or not. And with Koeder, and his book *Learn to See, Learn to Draw,* I discovered someone who had gone to design school, yet no one there had ever explained to him how to draw. Both gave me a sense of possibilities and the realization I wasn't alone in my frustration in trying to draw.

I don't want to overstate it, but now that I have some ability in drawing (and a bit in painting as well), I realize what a vital skill it is. Everything I do creatively—branding, photography, travel, furniture design, food presentation, interior or landscape design, and more—is better because sketching taught me to see better.

It took a change in perspective to get me to draw. And drawing has changed my perspective on so much of life. I just wish I had started this sooner.

CHAPTER 12
PERSPECTIVE

Where you learn how to reframe fear, suffering, success, and more, and how to develop your voice and style as a way to share your unique perspective.

There is no new truth, dear. All truth belongs to God. Sometimes you simply need to hear someone else say it. That's what I hope I'm doing for you. And that's what your voice will be for them.

— Emily P. Freeman, *A Million Little Ways*

Sometimes we forget that life is multifaceted. We perceive only one facet and believe there is only one story we can tell about it. When we forget about the multitude of viewpoints at our disposal, we don't consider ourselves storytellers at all. We just report the disappointing and immutable facts as we have learned them. But facts aren't stories. Stories are our interpretation of facts.

— William Kenower, *Fearless Writing: How to Create Boldly and Write with Confidence*

Of all the creative mindset tools in this book, Perspective may be the most mindsetty of the lot. Our ability to see any situation from a multitude of perspectives gives us the ability to not just rethink, but reset our reality. As writer Pico Iyer notes:

> ...it's not our experiences that form us but the ways in which we respond to them; a hurricane sweeps through town, reducing everything to rubble, and one man sees it as a liberation, a chance to start anew, while another, perhaps

even his brother, is traumatized for life. 'There is nothing either good or bad,' as Shakespeare wrote in Hamlet, 'but thinking makes it so.'[50]

The best news about perspective is that you can change yours. In fact, doing so—reframing—is the closest thing I know to a superpower. Is that glass half empty or half full? Rabbit or duck? It's all in how you look at it.

Jesus was a master of reframing. Just look at the Sermon on the Mount (Matthew 5-7) for ways he shifted people's perspectives on what it means to murder, commit adultery, treat your enemies, etc. He was reframing people's perspective on God. We can do the same thing through our creative work. But it starts with reframing our own perspectives first.

In its simplest form, reframing involves seeking a range of alternative views of a situation. For example, I once heard of a gifted actor who spoke at a marriage conference. He illustrated the importance of tone of voice by performing a dozen different renderings of the same four words: "What did you say?" These ranged from tender and hopeful to brutal and accusatory. Same words but the different approaches—and hence perspectives—changed their meaning.

Sometimes, context alone will do that for you. You see a seemingly aloof person differently when you know their spouse is in the hospital. You value an ordinary looking painting more when you realize it is by a famous artist. By practicing reframing intentionally, however, you uncover a multitude of possibilities available to you for every project. Each of us has agency and assets. We simply need to remember that and choose to see our situations from a place of opportunity and abundance. Reframing can seem like we're trying to convince ourselves of an alternative reality or give ourselves a glorified pep talk. But as people of faith, it's the opposite. It's allowing the Holy Spirit to remind us of the deeper truth, the reality of all that is available to us we're not seeing. Every single day. We can be like the elderly saint who, when asked at 95 how she was doing replied, "I am better than I feel."

REFRAMING SUFFERING

When I encounter hard situations, I sometimes use reframing in an escapist manner. I seek to find the silver lining without acknowledging in heartfelt ways the dark cloud. But I've learned instead that affliction, like stuckness, has value to us creatively and the role of perspective isn't to deny the pain, but to see it differently.

Suffering doesn't make us more creative. But it does connect us to less superficial emotions. We see things with a clarity that our happier selves lack or aren't willing to pursue. And since great art (and much of all creativity) is about the expression of emotion, the deeper the emotion, the more resonant or at least more authentic the work.

Practically, this means reframing adversity, looking not just for upbeat alternative perspectives, but for the deeper truth and creative sparks buried within. At such times, I not only ask, "Lord, what are you showing me here?" to find a way through the loss. But also, "What lesson, learning, emotion, or drive lies in the wreckage?" This is not a callous mining of tragedy for my own personal use. Instead, it's an awareness that this present difficulty isn't the end of the story. And that if I can pay attention in the pain, I may glean insights of value for later. Not just for my creative work, but to help others who may go through similar challenges. In a way, it's a reframing of Romans 8:28, reminding myself that God works together all things for my good. It may not be clear at this moment. But I can trust that goodness will come.

REFRAMING SUCCESS

Reframing helps in hard times, but also with the idea of success. In fact, stop for a minute and answer this: "To me, success creatively means _____?"

No, really. Stop and think through that.

Then try this. Ask God, "What does success creatively mean for me from your perspective?" This can be freeing, revealing, or troubling, depending on your view of God and how much your perspective differs when you frame the question this way.

A friend of mine once told me that in the sport of dog racing, the dogs used to chase a live rabbit. Apparently, the rabbit today is mechanical, not just from a humane perspective, but because of this: With the live rabbit, if it ever stumbled and the dog caught it, both were euthanized (or, at least, for the dog, taken away). The reason? To anthropomorphize it a bit, the dog's reaction to catching the rabbit was, "This is it? This is what I've been chasing?" And after that, they could never get the dog to run again. The end reward wasn't worth the effort. I have to review my creative priorities from time to time to make sure I'm chasing what matters.

Key to this is realizing that while I believe God calls us to do our best and to do all things as unto the Lord (Col. 3:23), I've stopped conflating *doing my* best with *being the* best.

When you look at the lives of people who are at the top of their game, the pinnacle of their field, their work *is* their world. The sacrifices of family, health, and other areas are extreme. Being excellent—but not number one in my field—gives me all the benefits of enjoying the work and its rewards without giving up other areas of my life.

Author Ryan Holiday captures this well:

The key then, when you find yourself wanting more, feeling inferior because you don't have more, is to think about that. Don't give the fantasies more weight than they deserve. See them for what they are. When you find yourself pining for fame and recognition, stop and consider what it might actually feel like when you get it...This is not to say you must be poor or a failure. You can still be extraordinary. You just don't have to be the most extraordinary. You don't have to strive to beat out all the other broken people, to be the most well-known out of everyone who ever wanted to be known. Because what is that actually worth in the long run? Do you think you'll appreciate your fame and money after you die? You think Alexander the Great knows that Alexandria is still standing?[51]

COMPROMISING ON QUALITY

Personally, I've never come close to being the best in the world at anything other than being me. But I do have to worry about my perspective in the other direction.

A few years ago, my son Sumner, then in his early 20s, and I traveled to China expressly to experience art and design there. We not only explored ancient and contemporary examples of design throughout China, but we also devoted time to our own art making. I was just beginning to take sketching seriously and spent many hours in each place doing so. Then, at the Dali airport waiting for our flight to Shanghai, I noticed my sketchbook page was not completely opaque. I found that if I took a photo on my phone and held the phone up to the paper, I could see enough of the image to trace the outlines. I only wanted the rough reference points to start the sketch with the correct linear perspective (oh, so many ways to use this word).

I shared my discovery with Sumner. He looked at me as if I'd informed him I was a camel, and responded with equal measures of disbelief and compassion, "You could do that, Dad, but why?" My head tilted like a dog deciphering a strange command. He continued, "Why rob yourself of the pleasure and even worshipful experience of drawing the whole thing?"

To be honest, it took me a while to get what he was saying. Why wouldn't you want to speed up the process? Until, suddenly, my perspective shifted faster than a politician's position on an unpopular issue. I realized how right Sumner was, how I had been thinking in terms of efficiency and outcome and had missed the value of presence, prayer, mastery, and a deeper appreciation of the process. I had been compromising in small ways that could become big issues later. And as we shall see in a later chapter, this wasn't the last time one of my sons would call me out on this issue.

PERSPECTIVE AND VOICE/STYLE

So far, everything has been about how you can shift your perspective for you. Let's now shift toward how your creative work reflects your unique perspective to others.

I haven't covered the topics of voice and style as much here since I do so more in my other book and course on *Branding for Artists and Creatives*. But briefly, your creative voice and style are your primary ways of communicating your perspective to the world. People often use these terms interchangeably. For our purposes, I will define voice as relating to the distinctive way you write and speak and style as your unique approach to portraying things visually. You can detect the difference in voice by comparing contemporaries such as Ernest Hemingway (terse sentences) and William Faulkner (whose sentences can take up whole paragraphs). And for style, just look at a portrait by Rembrandt versus one by his contemporary, Vermeer. You can immediately tell who painted what because of their different styles.

In my branding work, we say that your content or messaging is what you say, but your voice is how you say it. And in today's noisy world, *how* you say something matters as much or more than what you say. This is why voice and style are so important. You can cover the same topics or paint the same subjects as others and still stand out because of your unique way of seeing the world.

It takes time to refine your voice and style, but we all have a head start because we all have personalities (despite what the sales staff in a company I once worked for claimed about its engineers). Both style and voice stem from personality and thus, if you're struggling to define your unique approach, start with making a list of your key personality characteristics. You only need a few to capture who you are.

Similarly, you don't need to say much to convey your perspective, personality, and hence, your voice. Hector Garcia, in his book, *The Magic of Japan*, provides a great example of this from another book, *Taiko* by Eiji Yoshikawa:

> Early in the book, the following lines show the personalities of these three key figures in the history of Japan:
>
> What happens if the bird doesn't sing?
>
> 'Kill it!' replies Oda Nobunaga.
>
> 'Make it want to sing,' replies Hideyoshi Toyotomi.
>
> 'Wait,' replies Tokugawa Ieyasu.[52]

It was Tokugawa who finally united all of Japan after 150 years of internal conflict and brought peace to the country. He could see Japan from a perspective that others couldn't. It only takes one word from him to reveal that.

SEEING FROM MULTIPLE POINTS OF VIEW

We've seen how you can reframe your own perspective on suffering, success, or perceived failure, or share that perspective with others through your personality, voice, and style. Now, let's return to the heart of perspective and how the same situation can have different meanings when viewed from different perspectives. It's not just something to be aware of, but an important asset to use for creating adventurously.

One of my favorite examples of this comes from the FX show, *The Bear*. It's about a Michelin-starred chef who returns to his brother's Chicago sandwich shop upon the death of the brother. The whole arc of the second season is how to transform this run-down fast-food equivalent dive into a fine dining establishment. If you haven't seen it, be aware that the language is saltier than the corned beef. But the storylines in some episodes are brilliant.

In one such episode, one of the staff, Richie, gets to intern with the best restaurant in the country, also in Chicago. Richie, now nearing middle age, has been a lost soul all his life. He sees this internship as just another dead end forced on him by others.

Through this episode, we see how this restaurant runs with incredible efficiency. A five-second delay gets one staff a stern reprimand and shaming before dozens of other employees. A sign under a clock in the kitchen reflects this focus on precision and timeliness. The sign reads, "Every Second Counts."

In the pivotal scene, we see how Richie, through the hard work and respect shown at this restaurant, has transformed. He now senses both an opportunity and responsibility to do something with his life. He wanders into the restaurant kitchen early one morning and finds a woman already there. We're not sure who she is at first. But soon we learn she (a cameo by Oscar-winner Olivia Coleman) is the lead chef and founder of the restaurant. And what is she doing? Peeling mushrooms. He asks her why. She replies it's because diners realize that someone had to do this by hand. There's no machine that can peel a mushroom. It adds to the handmade exquisiteness of the experience. Richie then asks why *she's* doing it and not an assistant. She replies, "Respect. Feels attached. Time spent doing this is time well spent." And as the scene ends, the camera returns to the sign under the clock.

As a viewer, you have this powerful aha realization of how the same words can mean many things. "Every second counts" isn't just a productivity reminder. It's a clarion call to Richie that he can still make something exceptional of his life. And for the rest of us, it's a notice to pay attention to the small things, the equivalent of each peeled mushroom. That wonder and goodness lie before and around us. And that each moment matters because each is filled with all the possibilities of life. Every second *counts*.

It's a great illustration of how much such small moments can shift our own perspectives, which can have a profound effect on our creative work and lives. Sometimes these moments of reframing happen to us. But what makes reframing a superpower is that more often, it's a tool, a choice we get to make. It takes effort to do so. And it takes time.

But that is time well spent.

QUESTIONS AND EXPLORATIONS

- Think back on a past perceived failure. Then list how many good things have come about because of it.
- What does "time well spent" look like for you? What could you give up or rearrange to focus on activities that are time well spent?
- In *Hidden Travel* I wrote, "Scott Adams, creator of the comic strip *Dilbert*, notes that most of us will never be the best in the world at any one thing. But if you can be better than 75% of people in two or more fields, you've got a niche. Adams admits he's not the funniest person, but he's funnier than 75% of the population. And is he the greatest artist? No. But he can draw better than three-quarters of us. Put those two skills together, humor and drawing, and you've got a great cartoonist."[53] In what two or more areas are you better than 75% of people? What might that look like if you combined those areas? Don't settle for one answer. Pursue different combinations until you find some mix that resonates and that you can do extraordinarily, even if you're not the best in the world at it.

PLACE: *PHOTOGRAPHY*

I learned the basics of photography in high school. But it wasn't until I was teaching a business program in China for a year after grad school that photography became a passion. Part of that was due to a visiting lecturer, Stan Belland, who came to China to teach with me for several weeks. Every day after class, we'd be off on bikes exploring and taking photos of various parts of Tianjin, the city where I lived.

Stan gave me two things, both indirectly. The first was an appreciation of the infinite possibilities of photographing people and an understanding of darkroom techniques. The second was his daughter. Maybe "gave" sounds too old-fashioned. He *invited* me to his house in Southern California for dinner after we both returned from China and his daughter, Kris, just happened to be there. A year and a half later, we were married. It's a long story, but a good one.

On all the trips I've made with Kris since then, I don't think there's been one in which I didn't have a camera. One of my sons once asked me, "Why don't you take a trip and leave your camera at home? You might enjoy the trip more." Interpretation: *he'd* enjoy the trip more without Dad always taking pictures. But I considered his question, then realized that no, I wouldn't enjoy it as much. Because making photos is, for me, part of the experience of a location. I can't separate the two. It's not about the photo or the place. It's about both.

Most of my travel friends don't get this. They think I'm missing out by seeing the place only through a camera lens. Most of my photographer friends totally get this. They understand that photography is more than documenting your experience or showing others on Instagram what a great time you're having. It's not seeing less by viewing it through a camera lens. It's seeing more, just as in sketching, by focusing on details I'd otherwise miss.

Most of all, I'm actively engaging my creative skills—particularly my improvisational ones—in places of great beauty and interest. To me, as with fly fishing, that increases the joy of both.

CHAPTER 13
PLACE

Where you leverage your environment for greater creative satisfaction and flow.

The first thing painters ask about a studio-space usually concerns the light. And so one might think of a studio as a kind of conservatory or observatory or even lighthouse. And of course light is important. But it seems to me that a studio, when being used, is much more like a stomach. A place of digestion, transformation and excretion. Where images change form. Where everything is both regular and unpredictable. Where there's no apparent order and from where a well-being comes.
— **John Berger, *The Shape of a Pocket***

The value of life does not depend upon the place we occupy. It depends upon the way we occupy that place.
— **Therese of Lisieux**

I have the best wife in the world. Maybe the entire universe. Except when she does one mundane thing.

She moves my stuff.

And then, the word unhappy doesn't even touch how I feel.

Yes, she has allowed our living and dining rooms to look like a crazed photo shoot with all the lighting equipment and artifacts for the various Creativity Boxes you see between each chapter. And, okay, so my watercolor supplies are scattered here and there. And sure, she corrals my mail and various craft-projects-in-the-making that otherwise pile up in the kitchen. Oh, and did I mention her tolerance for the 30-40 library books I routinely have stacked by my chair in the family room? She's wonderfully accommodating most of the time. Until we have company. And then, she moves all those piles.

And I see red.

Don't ask creative people to be logical about their tools or materials. And don't mess with anything they consider to be their creative place. Even if, technically, it's a shared space that belongs to others just as much.

The smallest slot for a tool or the largest studio, it doesn't matter. We don't like anyone messing with our stuff or our space.

Place matters creatively because we are both physical and spiritual beings. As I noted earlier in Chapter 5, Environment, where you are, affects who you are. The key question is, how can we use place in positive ways to create adventurously and do our best work?

To answer that, I'll focus here on three that are most relevant to you, the adventurous creative:

- How to use place as a safe space to focus and embrace routines.
- How to use travel and unfamiliar places as a disruptor of those routines so you can get distance and see things anew.
- How to find the places that lie somewhere in between, places where you delight in this wondrous combination of doing something you love in a special location.

Are you in a good place to start? Let's go.

PLACE AS A SAFE SPACE

We need safe places to create. You may read many novels with battle scenes, but you don't read any written during a battle. We need some places in our creative lives that are akin to the Spanish term, *querencia*. It comes from the world of bullfighting and refers to the place in the ring—it could be anywhere the bull chooses—where the bull returns to when feeling threatened. It's thus a physical place in the bullring and a psychological space for the bull. And once that bull gets into its *querencia,* it is both difficult and dangerous for the matador to lure the bull away from there.

We each need our own *querencia* from which we can create. For many, this will be your atelier or studio, your dedicated writing space, your office or kitchen or she-shed. It could be a corner of your bedroom or a library carrel. Whatever you call it, you need some place of safety you can return to. You also need the corresponding structures and routines associated with it to produce great creative work consistently. For without these things, it will be hard to maintain the openness and even systems that are core to creating adventurously over time.

When I was first married and living in a small apartment, our kitchen/dining/living area served multiple creative purposes since it was all we had. Now, as an empty nester, I've co-opted multiple nooks in our home for doing different types of creative work. I used to think that was unusual until I read how and where other creatives over time have worked. In *Conceptual Blockbusting,* James L. Adams notes:

In his book, The Art and Science of Creativity, *George Kneller discussed the sometimes bizarre devices many writers and artists have adopted with respect to their working environment: 'Schiller, for example, filled his desk with rotten apples; Proust worked in a cork-lined room; Mozart took exercise; Dr. Samuel Johnson surrounded himself with a purring cat, orange peel, and tea; Hart Crane played jazz loud on a Victrola.' To these people, these steps were aids to the intense concentration required in creative thinking. As another example, an extreme case was Immanuel Kant, who would work in bed at certain times of the day with the blankets arranged around him in a way he had invented himself.*[54]

I've tried my own blanket configuration: It's done more for my sleep than my creativity.

Various studies have looked at factors that enhance creativity in different spaces. But—no big surprise—it comes down to finding what works for you. For some, facing into a room promotes creativity. Others find staring at blank walls most helpful. Others like to look out a window or decorate their space with inspiring images, swatches, and artwork. The items on your wall can be works by others, your own work to remind you of past accomplishments, notes from fans or press clips to affirm you, or even devotional aids to help you abide with Jesus creatively. Whatever helps. It's your wall, after all.

Non/low-stimuli environments work well for deep concentration. For some. While research shows that multitasking is to creative concentration what water is to cats, some people concentrate better with some stimuli (e.g. music, artwork, other people, nature). Distracting environments can also assist divergent thinking, where pinging from idea to idea can be a good thing.[55] It comes down to finding the right setting for you. For this project. For this day. That's because some days you're sensitive to things that other days you ignore. A noisy coffee shop doesn't faze me one day, but the next, a single crow cawing a block away can wreck my concentration.

One thing that works for most people is going into nature or bringing it into your space (which is why I love making terrariums). Other factors to consider include noting which scents activate your creative juices. Or adjusting the temperature based on inspiration over comfort. Lofty ceilings and airy spaces seem to aid in concept development, whereas low ceilings and more intimate environments can make convergent thinking and editing easier. Curved walls and surfaces also promote creative ideas over straight ones.[56]

FIND THE SPACE THAT WORKS FOR YOU

The secret to finding or making your optimal creative space anywhere is (surprise!) experimentation. Start by doing a creative space audit. Note your emotions as you do certain types of work in different places. Don't just note the environmental cues such as light and sound. Note your feelings and what particular task or energy mode aligned best with that space. I have a specific armchair in our living room (with a high, vaulted ceiling) that I go to only for ideation sessions. There's a café inside a supermarket a mile from home that I turn to when I need to generate lists of ideas. I may sit on my bed when I first awaken and write and stand at a makeshift desk in another room in the afternoons to paint. I do all client calls and video meetings in yet another space.

You can keep your space messy or clean (my woodworking shop is usually messy, but my writing area is usually clean). What matters is that you can find what you need without effort and a space that aids the specific type of work you're doing. I should say spaces because, for me, it's more of an ecosystem of creative environments that align with my energy mode and the type of work to do. I also find I do manual work (sketching, woodworking, crafts, etc.) better in dedicated spaces that differ from where I do digital work on a computer. Part of it is ergonomics, but part is reinforcing the associations with one type of work over another.

When auditing your various spaces, ask yourself, both "What do I feel here?" and then, "What do I *want* to feel here?" or "What kinds of work feel right here?"[57] Concentration feels different from inspiration or productivity or connection to others. Learn where to go to feel what.

MAKE IT A SPACE OF RE-CREATION

When you find a particular location where you have breakthrough ideas, go there repeatedly *for that type of work.* Your brain is a pattern-making machine. It will associate that place with happy, creative thoughts. This helps because your shop/studio/atelier isn't just a place of inspiration and creation, but one of Re-creation and renewal. It's a physical reminder that you can do this again and again. This is why you want to guard such environments from negative associations. Don't do the tasks you hate, like paying bills or dealing with online trolls in your studio. Protect and preserve your studio as sacred space. Pray over it and acknowledge God's presence with you each time you go there. Do the same thing with your creative time. Guard it and your space as you do your heart, since they are so interconnected.

MAKING ROOM FOR DISRUPTIONS

You will need such safe, comfortable places to foster creativity, but you'll also want places of adventure and discomfort, something that disrupts routine.

One of the most surefire ways to disrupt that routine is through travel. Just look at the Bible. Some of the most pivotal moments for characters in that book happened on a journey. Abraham's adult life was nomadic. Jacob's wrestling with God occurred on his return to meet Esau. Moses' life direction changed at the burning bush. Daniel's, in exile. Paul's on the road to Damascus. And Jesus? He said of himself, "Foxes have holes and birds of the air have nests, but the Son of Man has nowhere to lay his head." (Matthew 8:20). There's something about the distance and disruption of being away from your norm that gets our attention and makes us more open to what God is saying and doing.

CREATIVITY AND TRAVEL

This is why, to me, creativity and travel go so well together: we pay better attention in novel situations. New places inspire us and force us out of our comfort zones and into using our improvisational creativity skills. As David Brooks puts it in *The Social Animal*: *When you explore a new landscape or visit a new country, your attention is open to everything, like a baby's. One thing catches your eye. Then another. This receptiveness can happen only when you are physically there. Not when you are reading about a place, but only when you are on the scene, immersed in it. If you don't actually visit a place, you don't really know it. If you just study the numbers, you don't know it. If you don't get used to the people, you don't know it. As the Japanese proverb puts it: Don't study something. Get used to it. When you are out there on the scene, you are plunged into particulars. A thousand sensations wash over you.*[58]

Those "particulars" become the raw materials you collect for inspiration and sometimes, for a particular project. Think about how much place serves almost as a character in many books or films. Imagine Joseph Conrad's Heart of Darkness taking place in rural Iowa. Or Indiana Jones occurring in a shopping mall. The stories just wouldn't be the same in different settings.

But trips can do even more.

I remember author and podcaster Joanna Penn telling me about a pilgrimage she'd made. She expected the experience to be a time of renewal: physical, emotional, mental, and creative. Instead, she found no ideas came to her on those long days of walking. She returned feeling disappointed she had collected no new creative sparks. Until two weeks after her return, when both new ideas and renewed vitality flooded over her. Thus, the rewards of distance aren't always immediately apparent.

The distance needed for creative insights, disruptions, and rejuvenation can involve long voyages that take weeks or could be an hour doing something different a mile from home. They can include doing a fun activity once a week just to refill your creative well. Or they can be more intentional efforts, like retreats, conferences, or residences. The key in all this is *different*. You are using the physicality of movement and the novelty of a new place—even one near where you live but have never visited—to accomplish things you simply can't do in your head or in a familiar environment.

FINDING PLACES OF CREATIVE JOY

A third way you can leverage place is to connect your creative work with a particular location to increase the joy of both. The best example I've found of this is working on a particular project in a delightful new environment. When you're doing something you love in a beautiful or special place, you increase the delight of both. The most obvious example, at least for visual artists, is sketching on location. You see the place better because you're paying closer attention by drawing it. And the sketch you make there is more memorable and enjoyable because you did it in a fascinating place. Here are two additional examples.

I spent my junior year of college studying in Germany. During that time, I also worked on a play for my senior honors project (I was a theater minor). I had long weekends the whole spring semester. So, armed with a set of Eurail passes, I spent a good deal of my time on trains going all over Germany and Western Europe. I'd use much of the travel time jotting down ideas for the plot, snippets of dialog, or, since the play involved performing stage magic, designing illusions. The time spent on those trains was itself magical. It combined movement, making, novelty, and an ongoing sense of God being part of all of it.

A decade later, I spent a vacation with my wife and her family at a large house on the Hawaiian island of Kauai. I'd brought with me some woodcarving tools and a piece of basswood for carving a Santa. Not all creativity, after all, is fine art. Whenever we gathered outside, I'd carve. All the associations of that place are now tied to that one Santa (which I later gave to my niece, who was fascinated with the carving process). I multiplied the joy there by having time with family (pleasure 1), in a beautiful location (pleasure 2), and doing something with my hands creatively (pleasure 3).

When you make something on a trip, you imbue it with powerful emotions and associations. Whether you write your novel in Argentina or study cooking in Vietnam, combining making and place can transform both. You also return home with additional assets, energy, insights, and creative momentum because you engaged your creativity while you were away. Oh, and don't forget, you also bring home cooler souvenirs than you could ever buy.

CONNECTING ALL THREE

Most of the time these three ways of thinking about place—as a nurturing, safe location for getting work done; as a way of getting outside your routine to see things anew; and as a way of doing what you love in places you love—are mutually exclusive. But not always.

Sometimes when I'm on an airplane, I choose not to do email or connect to Wi-Fi or have any other distractions. I treat my airline seat as a safe, sacred space. It is a special time and place where God shows up in marvelous ways and makes whatever I'm working on more exciting and enjoyable.

In one case, I prayed for a creative breakthrough as I stared at a page of handwritten notes. And almost as in the movies, all the words on the page seemed to blur except two. And those two, while seemingly unrelated, turned out to be the answer I was praying for. In another instance, the airline's ad copy on the cocktail napkin had a word that unlocked a vast flow of ideas I'd never considered before. Breakthroughs like these aren't common. But they still serve as symbols or reminders of how God can use such places to unleash something in us that may never happen in our day-to-day spaces and routines.

Thus, place and space aren't just creative tools. They are objects of desire, geographic locations of wonder, markers of worship I look forward to and pursue. They are worthy of respect and response. Even ones that may not seem special. Because I never know what shrub might erupt in flame before me as I find myself struggling to kick off my sandals in a place that seemed so ordinary a moment before, yet now is anything but.

QUESTIONS AND EXPLORATIONS

- What is your *querencia* or place of safety? Do you go there too much or not enough?
- Exercise: Do a creative space audit to identify all the factors or environmental cues that make for your best work. Consider where (or under what conditions/circumstances) you best do different forms of creating: discover/ideate, create/connect, process/production, edit/refine, etc.
- Go to www.ExploreYourWorlds.com/Motivation and review the list of factors or moods that help or hinder my creating. Use that as a spark to make your own list of elements that affect you creatively. You can do this in your head or by writing, but the previous exercise works best if you can visit each location and see how physically being there influences or moves you.

OTHERS: *COOKING*

The beauty of cooking, for me, is to have a creative outlet that I know I will never monetize. Frankly, the idea of making the same dishes day after day for guests in a restaurant does not appeal to me creatively. But I am so glad it does to others. For a delicious meal, particularly with others, is one of life's great joys.

I'm an inventive cook: Tell me the few ingredients in the pantry or fridge and I can whip together something decent—or at least edible. I like recipes, but I treat them as starting points. This works in many cases, but in others, the precise instructions are there for a reason. Thus, I win some; I lose some. But mostly win.

The biggest win (besides being able to eat what I make) is in learning about food so that I can better appreciate meals made by others. It's a good reminder that the more you learn about any creative area, the more interesting it becomes as both your tastes (of all kinds) and judgment improve.

The main problem with my cooking is its singular focus on speed. My family jokes about me having my own cooking show on the Food Network. "Cooking with Steve" would be limited to dishes you can cook hot and fast. That essentially limits my culinary tools to a grill and a wok.

That's changed as I've learned the wonders of baking and the value of flavor layers which take long periods to build. But what hasn't altered for me is the alone/together nature of cooking.

I still love to make up new combinations of food just to appeal to my curiosity and hunger. But there are few activities that bring as much closeness and delight as a shared meal. Which is why I'm so thankful to be married to an extraordinary cook. When we entertain, Kris usually does most of the cooking. That way, I get the benefit of dining with friends and those friends get something other than grilled meat and vegetables or stir fry.

CHAPTER 14
OTHERS

Where you find greater purpose and joy in using your creativity for and with others.

If you want happiness for an hour, take a nap. If you want happiness for a day, go fishing. If you want happiness for a year, inherit a fortune. If you want happiness for a lifetime, help somebody.

— Chinese Proverb

I have evolved a credo: 'Always think of my audience, but never think for my audience.' Even so, occasionally I get this funny feeling...I yearn to make something that is purely mine, free from any restrictions, without regard for those who will eventually see it. This feeling is an affliction every 'creative type' suffers through to a greater or lesser degree. In small doses, it's called having 'an artistic vision'; in larger doses, it's known as having 'zero commercial potential.'

— Mo Willems, *Don't Pigeonhole Me!*

My second-most favorite moment in a branding or innovation workshop with clients comes at the end. It happens when we've landed on a concept, and everyone loves it. My most favorite moment is when no one can remember where the idea came from.

The rich interaction, the contributions from all the team members, the cascading of concepts—it all blurs. The result is better than any of us could have done individually. And yet, that same result wouldn't have happened had we not taken the time, as part of the workshop, to process and ideate individually as well as in the group sessions.

To create adventurously means to embrace a rhythm of making that encompasses both solitude and community, time alone and time together. The secret is to find the right mix of each: for you, for this season or project, and for those you work creatively for and with.

CREATING ON YOUR OWN

Making something alone, just for me, can fuel my creativity and help me refine my creative voice. It can provide the space I need to learn and try new things, to experiment, and to make bad first drafts. In solitude, I can listen better to my heart and God's, as well as to what the work may be saying. I can go deep into it without distraction and hold onto it with better clarity.

For me, and I suspect you, I need time alone to focus, go deep, and to hold multitudes of ideas, worlds, and emotions together in my head. Without solitude, I let distractions win and others define me. Solitude is like the negative space of a painting. What's not there clarifies what is. Solitude, however, can be especially hard for people who confuse aloneness with loneliness. But even the ache of absence can sharpen one's senses and lead to surprising insights and breakthroughs.

I spend far more time working alone than I do with others. As an introvert, I prefer it that way. Until I remember that my best work *always* happens when it involves other people. And the way I do this is through a combination of *with* and *for* others.

CREATING TOGETHER WITH OTHERS

Working *with* others can mean inviting trusted critique partners or advisers to speak into my work. It can also include like-minded and like-hearted collaborators who pull off more than I could on my own. They share the burden, support and stretch me, understand why all this crazy creative stuff means so much to me, and fill in gaps in my skill set. When working with others, I'm not just making art. I'm hopefully making friends as well. After all, one of the greatest things we can create is community.

We work with others more experienced than us to improve our abilities. We work with those less experienced to improve theirs. You can be the mentor or the mentee or, as I've found, a bit of both since I constantly learn from those I seek to mentor. In either case, iron sharpens iron: Sometimes you're the blade, and sometimes you're the sharpening steel. And sometimes you're not sure who is which.

You can also work with others by getting and providing feedback and support. This can include an advanced readers' group you send your draft novel to, a collective of other artists or people in your field that you meet with regularly, a more structured group like a regular critique group, or simply a set of colleagues. Even a loose network of other creatives you meet online or at conferences counts.

Where possible, I always strive for as much diversity in people and responses as I can get. For example, in any visual design project for my branding clients, I review a new deliverable with both my business and the creative teams. If only one side loves it, back it goes for refinement. When both sides love it, I know we can present it with confidence to the client. Not listening to both perspectives, business and creative, is like operating with half a brain.

With a critique group, variety helps, but even better is having members who strive to up the excellence of everyone in the group. In healthy groups, particularly with people of faith, there's a spirit of goodwill and shared purpose that goes beyond mere encouragement. They want me and my work to succeed, not just for my sake, but for God's. In such groups, we pray for each other and over each other's work. We seek to point out what is working, not just what needs improvement. We don't merely support each other; we *get* each other.

Working in such groups makes me realize that my creative skills may, in the long run, make a greater difference in the world through the thoughtful support I give others in their work. A few well-chosen comments to another author may cause their book to take off in ways mine never will. And that may be the entire reason I'm there. I came to critique groups looking for what I could get out of them. Now I look forward to how much I can give.

Your critique group and other forms of community—even if it is only two of you—serve the three functions that creativity expert Todd Henry notes are essential to creating well:

The key to cultivating creatively stimulating relationships is threefold: you need relationships in your life in which you can be real, you need relationships in your life in which you can learn to risk, and you need relationships in your life in which you can learn to submit to the wisdom of others.[59]

This wisdom of others often comes not in telling us something new, but in reminding us of what we already knew but forgot.

HELPING EACH OTHER TO REMEMBER

Years ago, my wife, sons, and I attended a Young Life family camp in Eastern Oregon. The closing service was powerful. The pastor recognized how meaningful it had been and cautioned us to keep thinking about what had moved us as we drove home.

He said that by the time we got back to Portland (four hours away) or Seattle (seven hours away), or wherever we lived, without effort, we will have forgotten all that God was saying to us in our time at camp.

I mentioned this to my friend Dave, a psychologist, several weeks later. He laughed. I asked why. He said that of course I will have forgotten the message. To think otherwise is to not understand humans. Our brains aren't built for remembering, but for problem solving. Memory simply aids in that. Thus, we are prone to forget. It's one reason scholars and others often refer to the Bible as a book of remembering. But he noted this: "That's why we have each other."

We need each other creatively, not just to help us look forward to what might be, but to recall what has been and to see what is. To remind us of what we already know, but have mislaid or let go dormant. About who we are, who God is, and how much our work matters.

CREATING TOGETHER FOR OTHERS

Besides working with some amazing creatives, I also get to work *for* others. This means serving, celebrating, blessing, and hopefully delighting my audiences. My primary goal is to understand their needs and their dreams and create work that addresses both. I try to listen to them, but also realize that what they say and what they *want* are rarely the same. This quote, attributed to Henry Ford, comes to mind: "If I'd listened to my customers, I would have built a faster horse." I want to serve my audience and provide something of value. But determining how is up to me alone. David Bowie captured this tension well: "I think it's terribly dangerous for an artist to fulfill other people's expectations—they generally produce their worst work when they do that." So how do we serve our audiences without being driven by them? By understanding what they want, then delivering something they could never have imagined on their own.

A DIFFERENT APPROACH TO MARKETING

This starts with seeing your audiences in what may be a new way. Let's be honest. Most of us love making the work, but marketing or selling it? Can't someone else do that for us? Unfortunately, no. But it doesn't have to be as painful as you may think.

Author Karen Barnes first introduced me to seeing platform building—all that stuff you do to build an audience—not as an act of marketing, but as one of love. If you picture each person in your audience as someone you serve and want to bless, rather than someone you're trying to convince to buy your work, it transforms how you'll share and sell that work.

Another practical perspective on this comes from book marketer Tim Grahl. He defines marketing, at least for authors (and I'd say most creatives as well) in two simple points:

1) Focus on long-term relationships. You're not here to sell just this book, but the seventh book from now.

2) Be relentlessly helpful.

These are helpful points because of this: Making creative work is rarely scary. Sharing that work with others is. We put so much of ourselves into our creative efforts and then expose the results to the world. That vulnerability can pay off when people respond to your authenticity. Or the process can crush you when they ignore, misinterpret, or reject the work (and thus, it feels, reject you as a person). The high risk here can deter you from making anything at all. Or it can lead you to pursue "a still more excellent way."

When I create not just out of grace, but out of love, I overcome much of the anxiety that comes from sharing my creative work with others. As we saw earlier, it is a fine line between thinking, "I just don't care what others think" to "I am making this as a gift for them, but how they react is their issue." I care what they think. But I can't control that. What I can do is care enough to understand their needs *before* I make something for them.

Understanding their wants and needs before I engage in the work for them differs from constantly wondering if they will like it, as I'm making it. The former, a form of research or preparation, fuels my curiosity. The latter merely distracts.

When I see my work through the lens of love and grace, when I see it as a gift to my audiences, it frees me from so much fear. I can still be disappointed if people don't react well to my work. I'm not sure that ever goes away completely. But the key here is that creating from grace and love enables me to *make* that work without the constant concern at every step of "will this be good enough?" or "am I good enough?" I shift my focus to the joy of making something for others with Jesus and trust him to take care of the rest.

POURING YOURSELF OUT FOR OTHERS

One of my favorite examples of creating for others comes from the film *Babette's Feast*. In it, two elderly sisters, daughters of the pastor of a small Puritan-like congregation in Norway, have both sacrificed to live pious lives as their now-deceased father would have wanted. One day, a woman, Babette, shows up on their doorstep with a note from an old suitor of one sister. In the note, he requests they take in Babette, who is destitute after having fled Paris when her family was killed during the French civil war in the late 19th century. The note ends with three words: "Babette can cook." And she does. For twelve years, she prepares simple meals for the two sisters and adjusts to life in the Norwegian village.

Then one day, she receives notification that she has won the French lottery. She asks the sisters the first favor of her entire time there: Can she prepare a dinner in honor of the 100th anniversary of the sisters' father's birth? Eventually, the sisters accept. Soon, shipments arrive of exotic foods, wines, and ingredients. Eventually, in the pivotal scene of the dinner, the sisters, and the few remaining congregants that have gathered, begin the meal with decades-old resentments and petty squabbles. But during the dinner, a transformation occurs. They confess to and forgive each other. We learn

Babette was once the most famous chef in Paris. And by the end, we realize it isn't an act of severe piety that has saved this small congregation. It is Babette's extravagant act of generosity and artistry.

Afterwards, the two sisters ask Babette if she will now take her remaining lottery proceeds and use them to return to France. They are shocked to learn that nothing remains. Babette has used her small fortune to make this one meal.

Was it worth it? Was Mary pouring the expensive perfume on Jesus worth it? If we count our creative assets like financial ones, we'll always be considering our creative efforts in economic terms. That leads to a zero-sum way of thinking that will forever be biased toward scarcity. But if you see what you have been blessed with as something that multiplies as you give it away, your world changes. Just as it did for the characters in *Babette's Feast*.

You can't out-give God. And while we can do much on our own to glorify him, our most tangible expressions come when we make things on behalf of others. There will always be our fears of economic loss or hardship. That we can't afford to be so generous. That we have families to feed. Responsibilities to maintain. The usual. But this isn't about being a good steward or not. It's recognizing that our creativity plays by a different set of rules than our finances. That the gift of our creative abilities doesn't run out when we pour it out for others. It grows.

I have always loved these much-quoted words from author Annie Dillard:

> One of the things I know about writing is this: spend it all, shoot it, play it, lose it, all, right away, every time. Do not hoard what seems good for a later place in the book or for another book; give it, give it all, give it now. The impulse to save something good for a better place later is the signal to spend it now. Something more will arise for later, something better. These things fill from behind, from beneath, like well

water. Similarly, the impulse to keep to yourself what you have learned is not only shameful, it is destructive. Anything you do not give freely and abundantly becomes lost to you. You open your safe and find ashes.[60]

We can give completely because we do not navigate The Creative Wild alone. We are each a part of something so much bigger. We are blessed to take part in what God is doing in this world through, for, and with us, so we can do the same for others. Our creativity, when given and used for others, expands to make a difference in ways we may never realize.

Kevin Ashton, whom we met earlier, captures this well:

We are all connected, and we are creative. No one does anything alone. Even the greatest inventors build on the work of thousands. Creation is contribution. We cannot know the weight of our contribution in advance. We must create for creation's sake, trust that our creations may have impacts we cannot foresee, and know that often the greatest contributions are the ones with the most unimaginable consequences.[61]

QUESTIONS AND EXPLORATIONS

- Which gives you greater joy, coming up with a new idea on your own, or sharing the result with your audience? What is it about each that you most and least like?
- In her book *Bandersnatch*, Diana Pavlac Glyer tells of how C. S. Lewis encouraged J.R.R. Tolkien to write *The Lord of the Rings* even when everyone else dismissed the work. Lewis was, as she puts it, a "resonator," a committed champion to Tolkien. Who is a resonator in your life? Have you thanked them lately? To whom can you be a resonator?
- Recall that "making creative work is rarely scary, but sharing that work with others is." How might seeing your work as an act of grace that blesses others make sharing it less scary?

INDIRECTION: *GARDENING AND LANDSCAPE DESIGN*

Gardening and Landscape Design is a clunky creative category and an inadequate one. I enjoy gardening, but more the initial design and planting than the ongoing maintenance. I find it remarkably satisfying to create a pleasing arrangement of living things.

What I most love are terrariums and indoor plant arrangements. I've only built a few of the latter, but I have designs for an array of tables and wooden boxes, houses, and other forms with carefully crafted tops that have holes in one or more surface for the plants' stems, shoots and branches. The appearance is as if the plants are growing from either the tabletop or the top of a box or pyramid or other part of the object.

I guess you could call them planters, but I see them more as furniture or sculpture that incorporates living elements.

Same with terrariums. I love them because they are miniature worlds. Sometimes, I'll focus on the container. One of my favorites is made from two brass and beveled glass hall lights I repurposed (flipping one upside down and placing it over the other to create a closed environment that looks almost like a miniature Victorian greenhouse). Other times, I'll take a simple fishbowl and focus on the arrangement inside.

None of these is earth shattering. But it doesn't matter. They add greenery and an architectural touch to the rooms of our house. The only downside is keeping them all watered, but good terrarium design minimizes the frequency of this. Terrariums are an indirect way of bringing nature closer and are a good reminder of just how much lies beyond our control, such as how plants grow. We can only take an indirect approach to growing: water, fertilize, and otherwise tend the plants. The rest is up to God and nature.

CHAPTER 15
INDIRECTION

Where you learn to create more effectively by pursuing your goals and innovative ideas in less direct ways.

Poetry is the kind of thing you have to see from the corner of your eye. You can be too well prepared for poetry. A conscientious interest in it is worse than no interest at all, as I believe Frost used to say. It's like a very faint star. If you look straight at it you can't see it, but if you look a little to one side, it is there … If you analyze it away, it's gone. It would be like boiling a watch to find out what makes it tick …If you let your thought play, turn things this way and that, be ready for liveliness, alternatives, new views, the possibility of another world — you are in the area of poetry … Anyone who breathes is in the rhythm business; anyone who is alive is caught up in the imminences, the doubts mixed with the triumphant certainty, of poetry.
— William Stafford, *Writing the Australian Crawl*

Happiness may come at us face-to-face, but joy always comes at us at an angle.
— Adam Gopnik, *The Table Comes First*

Poets and artists don't define. They don't even describe, not completely. They use simile and metaphor to compare, evoke, and make us realize our experiences, while entirely our own, are shared by others. It takes the artist to express the inexpressible in emotions rather than definitions. Poets and artists understand that the direct path, while seeming to be the shortest is, in The Creative Wild, rarely the best. A truer, more reliable approach is the way of Indirection.

Aristotle said that "Nature operates in the shortest way possible." And yet, it's interesting that in nature, there are few straight lines. I often hunger for the shortest way, the direct path. But as C.S. Lewis noted, "'The longest way round is the shortest way home' is the logic of both fable and faith." And also, I have found, of creativity.

Indirection means pursuing what you seek in less obvious ways. As artist Bert Dodson notes in *Keys to Drawing with Imagination,* "Creativity is a lot like happiness. It shows up when you're thinking of something else."[62] Indirection is one of the many places where the worlds of creativity and productivity vary. With productivity, you seek the quickest means to reach your goal. With creativity, you find what you seek in the meandering journey. It's in the moments where you may feel most lost that you discover what the work most wants you to find.

I like how *Wired* magazine co-founder Kevin Kelly puts it: "Ask anyone you admire: Their lucky breaks happened on a detour from their main goal. So embrace detours. Life is not a straight line for anyone."[63]

The indirect route almost always takes longer and can feel like a waste of time. But remember the secret of hot streaks: explore then exploit. Many explorations can feel aimless until they provide substantial rewards later.

As with all the paradoxes in The Creative Wild, the opposite can also be true: sometimes direct is good. Sometimes gimmicks and short cuts help. Productivity is something we should pursue. But at the right time and in the right way. Too often, I find I attempt productivity hacks and shortcuts when I'm frustrated and just want the project done. But that doesn't lead to my best work. Instead, these attempts to save time usually reveal themselves to be false economies and hurt in the long run. I've cut corners and haven't become the person who the harder, less comfortable, and indirect route would have made me to be. You don't see Jesus taking the easy way out. In fact, he most harshly rebukes Peter ("Get behind me, Satan") when Peter suggests Jesus take a shortcut rather than going to the cross. (Matthew 16:23).

THE INDIRECT EFFECTS OF WHAT YOU DO

Indirection shows up in many forms. Jokes work because they are surprising, and they surprise because they are indirect. The direct approach to a photograph is a snapshot, but an indirect image can startle us into seeing a familiar place anew. Memorable stories get to the climax in an indirect way that seems inevitable. Taking a shower is a familiar, indirect way to generate new ideas.

A less familiar example happened several years ago when my family—parents, wife, and two sons—vacationed in Yellowstone National Park. My dad was then in his 80s, had macular degeneration (limiting his eyesight) and had some difficulty walking. Still, my sons and I were determined to get him out fishing, something he used to love to do. We found a spot along the Firehole River where the bank wasn't far from a pullout on the road. We helped him use his walker to get to the river, where he then sat on the walker. I hooked up his line with a casting bubble and a dry fly and off he went. He may not have been able to see clearly, but he could feel the tug when a fish was on the line.

To me, fly-fishing not only is creative, but a great example of Indirection. You rarely cast your fly directly in front of the fish (trout, in this case). That would be like sitting at your dining table and a huge ribeye steak suddenly appears before you. You'd suspect something fishy about that. Same with a fly appearing before you if you were a trout (though I doubt you'd use the term "fishy" in that case). Instead, casting the fly upstream and letting it drift in front of the fish—the indirect approach—gets better results.

But another, more powerful, example of Indirection came later when a minivan pulled up behind ours and just stopped there. We weren't sure what they were doing until a woman around my age came down to talk to my dad. I wandered over and heard her asking him how old he was and other rather odd questions. It turned out her own father was sitting up in the van. She'd seen my dad fishing from his walker and was so inspired that he'd be out there like that. She wanted her dad to see that he, too, could do something like this. You'd have thought we'd given her an incredible present, judging from her enthusiasm. And maybe we did, because my dad's example had apparently ignited hope and possibility in her father.

It was an indirect gift. But here's the best part. The rest of the time out there, my dad sat a little taller in his walker. Cast his fly farther. He even moved faster when it was time to walk back to the car. The indirect gift was not just the effect that his example had provided to the woman's father. It was the realization for my dad that he still could give such a gift to others.

And if you're thinking, that's a pleasant story, but how does it relate to creativity? Consider this: Some of the most important things you can ever make are experiences for others. We had to improvise (that often-overlooked form of creativity) to find a place for my dad to fish and to get him out there. But we knew it would mean a lot to him. We just never realized how much. And in the curious yet marvelous way God works, particularly through creating experiences for others, we rarely can know ahead of time the indirect blessings we can provide.

USING INDIRECTION AS A CREATIVE TOOL

Let me return now to more direct ways of using Indirection as a creative tool. Whatever your medium or work, here are some other indirect approaches you can try and questions to ask yourself as you create:

- "What are five other ways I could solve this problem? Ten? 50?" That can seem daunting but if you shift from seeking the "best" answer to seeking as many answers as possible, even crazy ones, you're able to produce far more results. And out of quantity comes quality. Remember: when you think you've exhausted all possibilities, keep going. That's when you get to the good, more indirect stuff.
- "What else could I do?" Once you find some strong possibilities, how could you enhance them? Add to them? Take away and simplify them?
- "What would I never do?" For example, I remember working with the team at Prophet, one of the world's top branding firms, for a client. They told of doing this exercise with Mattel and the Polly Pockets line of dolls for girls. When someone suggested "Polly Pockets Prostitute," everyone laughed and agreed they would *never* do that. But they kept pushing and thought, "If we did, what would that look like?" They realized they'd need a whole new line of child-friendly clothing for the dolls such as pajamas and other appropriate clothes the dolls could wear for sleepovers. The creation of these new outfits for the dolls has been a big hit with the young girls who buy Polly Pockets. So never hesitate to take a *very* indirect route by doing the opposite of what you'd normally consider.
- "What could I learn from _____?"[64] Let's say you're a landscape architect designing a garden within a city park. Ask yourself what you might learn from:
    - How Starbucks serves coffee
    - How Disneyland deals with lines and crowd control
    - How a mortuary deals with grieving families
    - How bees coordinate the activities of the hive
    - How children absorb themselves in play

Pretty indirect, right? But think through those. How might a landscape designer apply how Starbucks' baristas know ahead of time the orders of regulars? Or how could they apply the mortician's art of silence and pauses and creating space for emotions to a garden design? From Disneyland, the landscape designer could tap into the way you never see the full line for a ride and leverage the Japanese art of "*miegakure*" (translated as hide and reveal).[65] It's used in Japanese gardens where they lay out the paths so you can never see the full garden from any single point.

You likely could come up with many other indirect possibilities. But once you try this "What might we learn from _____?" exercise, it will likely become a staple because of how it forces you to consider more indirect approaches. Just be sure, as I've noted before, that you're solving for the right problem. In learning from others, you might discover that your original product, experience, or direction may not be what you really needed. For example, in the early days of NASA and the space race, US engineers spent hundreds of thousands of dollars trying to perfect a pen that could write in zero gravity. The Russians spent nothing. They used pencils.

INDIRECTION AND PROBLEM FINDING

Exploring alternative approaches from other professions or contexts (such as nature) can help in problem solving for known challenges, but also in problem *finding*. With the latter, you're looking for issues others haven't considered, improvements in the ways things have always been done. As Shelly Carson puts it in *Your Creative Brain*:

> *Problem finding does not mean that you go out looking for troublesome aspects of your life or work to criticize—we have bosses and mothers-in-law to do that job; it's more like exploring new ways that things could be done or could be done differently.*[66]

You could say that problem finding is upstream from problem solving. With the former, you widen your attention and curiosity to consider issues or opportunities before focusing on a specific problem to solve. The practice of design thinking involves a good amount of problem finding. With design thinking, you use empathy and listening to understand the needs of a particular audience instead of designing a product *you* determine on your own will meet those needs. You then take what you hear and reframe it in many ways to make sure you're addressing the right problem.

For example, let's say you discover that aspiring musicians in rural areas lack access to professional recording equipment. One possible solution would be to find ways to manufacture the equipment for less. But perhaps a better solution would be a form of musician co-ops to share existing equipment. Or even better, a mobile recording studio. You only know by considering a wide range of indirect options, then reviewing these through testing and prototyping with your audience in order to find the right solution.

Other examples of problem finding could include a medical researcher who notices links between nutrition and mental health in underserved populations and seeks out a range of nutritional options that are accessible to that community. Or an attorney who decides to build a new area of practice around ethical issues in the use of artificial intelligence. Or a painter who wants to explore a new style with her work. She can't "solve" that problem so much as find a new way of approaching her art.

INDIRECTION AND BEGINNER'S MIND

In addition to design thinking, another way to address problem finding and Indirection as a whole is by practicing Beginner's Mind. This approach helps you see a situation with fresh eyes so that your expertise doesn't blind you to new possibilities (which is what happened to the NASA engineers). When there's a single right answer or you need a quick solution for a known problem, expertise helps you to make quick decisions and avoid less effective possibilities, whether that's a doctor ruling out unlikely diagnoses or a master chess player eliminating the less-successful moves. But our expertise can also cause us to rule out a lot of creative ideas before we ever give them a chance to prove themselves.

With Beginner's Mind, you wander around the periphery of the problem and ask a lot of "stupid" or naïve questions to uncover the possibilities that the "curse of knowledge" has blinded the experts from seeing. As celebrated graphic designer Paula Sher notes:

When I'm totally unqualified for a job, that's when I do my best work...If you're trying to find a new way to think about something that makes it better, it can actually hurt you to have too much experience in that particular milieu—because you understand the expectations too well. And that can cause you to limit and edit your possibilities, based on what you already know 'doesn't work.'[67]

One way to get to Beginner's Mind is to try doing everything the opposite of what you've mastered. Try painting with the opposite hand. Try writing your topic but for a seven-year-old. Try taking elements from one area and using them in another. What could you apply from photography to songwriting? Or saddle-making to performance art? The goal is to break free of habits, both physical and mental, and find an indirect way to improve your craft.

SOME SUMMARIZING THOUGHTS ON INDIRECTION

Hopefully by now, you realize how powerful an indirect approach can be. Indirection lies at the heart of divergent thinking and is key to problem finding. Some of the artist's and writer's greatest tools are indirect ones: symbol, metaphor/analogy, irony, satire, ambiguity, layers of meaning, and hidden themes. Without Indirection, we make clunky, unimaginative propaganda that is so on the mark as to be off-putting or ignored.

Indirection is also a tool you can use when you're stuck. Instead of continuing (or trying to go) directly, you take a side road. You think like a beginner; you reset your expectations and approach. You can proceed directly when you know what you're doing and where you're heading. Indirection is for when you don't. It's a tool for rethinking or thinking in less obvious ways. That's the key.

I'd even go so far as to say that Indirection should be considered as more than just a tool, but an essential for all forms of creativity along with mastery, mindset, motivation, and environment. As George Orwell notes in Animal Farm, "All animals are equal. But some are more equal than others." So it is with Indirection. All these tools matter, but Indirection matters in more ways than most people realize.

If you want to make something beautiful, the ordinary won't do. You must adjust not just how you'll go, but where. Your category may be clear and direct (or maybe not), but what lies within it can be askew and indirect from what most people think. We don't want novels that take us to familiar destinations or paintings that don't surprise us. We want creative work that makes us see a familiar genre or medium as if we've experienced nothing like it before. And the pathway to get there is almost always an indirect one.

QUESTIONS AND EXPLORATIONS

- To practice Beginner's Mind, try this. Consider one area where you have expertise. Then, make a list of ten (or even five) things you would need to know if you were just starting in that area. Then try to practice those in an unfamiliar way (e.g., use your other hand, teach someone else, try a different genre, do it with your eyes closed, etc.).

- Think of an upcoming project. What's the root problem you're trying to solve? Are you sure? Keep asking yourself, "Is this it?" and pushing until you're sure of it. Then try an indirect way to solve it.
- Make a list of five roles or types of people you've never or rarely spoken to before. That might be a Jewish rabbi, an agricultural inspector, a person who manufactures ball bearings, a large-animal vet, or a podiatrist. Then, see if you could figure out what you might learn from each about a problem you're solving. It's great to meet them, but even considering your challenge hypothetically from their perspective can be an indirect way that opens a wealth of new possibilities.

INCOMPLETION: *MAGIC*

I worked as a professional magician from high school until a few years after college. Mostly I did private shows at homes, clubs, restaurants, and businesses. But I also spent three years as the lead demonstrator at Merlin's Magic Shop in Disneyland. It was the same place where I had purchased my first trick, the ol' Ball and Vase illusion (bottom right corner in the photo), several years earlier.

One day on the job there, one of the Jungle Cruise guides and I were having lunch. He asked why I loved magic. Was it for the performing aspect? I realized, probably for the first time, that it wasn't.

I loved coming up with new illusions or different ways of presenting old tricks. It was the compositional creativity of illusion design, not the improvisational creativity of performing, that appealed to me. I enjoyed the latter, but presenting the illusion before others was only a matter of proof of concept. Without performing the illusion, it would forever be incomplete in a bad way, a mere idea or a personal experience only (since it's pretty hard to fool yourself when practicing in front of a mirror).

The best performances of magic are models of Incompletion. If the audience figures out the trick, they have completion, but a shallow reward. When they don't, and even better, when they don't try to, they walk away having engaged in mystery. And that will almost always be more fulfilling in the long run than merely solving a puzzle.

I don't perform much anymore because most of what I did involved sleight of hand, and that takes a great deal of practice to maintain at a professional level. But the thinking behind both illusions and the presentation of them, along with the inherent wonder and mystery, all that stays with me and shows up in interesting ways in other creative projects to this day.

CHAPTER 16
INCOMPLETION

Where you learn what parts of your work to finish and what to leave undone so that audiences can complete it themselves for greater satisfaction.

I beg you, to have patience with everything unresolved in your heart and to try to love the questions themselves as if they were locked rooms or books written in a very foreign language. Don't search for the answers, which could not be given to you now, because you would not be able to live them. And the point is to live everything. Live the questions now. Perhaps then, someday far in the future, you will gradually, without even noticing it, live your way into the answer.
— Rainer Maria Rilke, **Letters to a Young Poet**

The thing about finishing a story is that finishing is really only the beginning.
— William Herring

When I see a work of art so beyond my skill level that I can't even figure out how to re-create it, I'm either inspired or depressed. I might feel amazed and appreciative of the work before me or somewhat hopeless that I will ever achieve such mastery.

But there is a third way.

I can choose to focus on what I can do, not what I cannot. On what is possible for me now, not what someone with years more experience has made. I can return to the work God has for me at this moment, in this place. And through it all, I can remind myself of the value of Incompletion.

I think the entire Christian life revolves around this tension of the now and the not yet. When my perspective shifts from what I can't do to what I can, I find peace. But there remains a desire to grow into the possibility of what I might make and even become one day. It's the contentment in the now combined with the yearning for what remains incomplete and lies ahead, even the eternal.

I remember a moment on my wedding day. I'd stepped aside at the reception just to rest a minute. And in that brief pause, I realized that the moment was a distillation of the best of life. Here I was, now married (as of a whole 90 minutes) to the woman I most loved with the people dearest to me surrounding us. The joy of that instant was exquisite. And yet, I knew that there was even more to come: the rest of the reception, the wedding night, the honeymoon, and coming home to live with my new bride for the rest of our lives. The sense of Incompletion, of the not yet, filled me with a delightful longing for what was to come even as I rejoiced in what was.

In our creative work, we will always be in some form of Incompletion. The Incubation stage of the creative process is all Incompletion. And even at the end of a massive project, there is still the next one to do. There's an ongoing sense of Incompletion in the cadence of tension and release inherent in making. But we're trained to see Incompletion as a negative. "Finish your homework." "Clean your plate." "Don't give up." "See this to the end." From youth, we're pressed with the value of completion and closure. Incompletion seems akin to failure. And yet, Incompletion is the hidden secret to finishing well in The Creative Wild.

As we saw earlier, perceived failures are usually matters of inadequate timeframes. So too with Incompletion. Every project is incomplete until it isn't. The solution is to find joy in the process. Appreciate the micro accomplishments. Don't stress that so much of the canvas remains blank, marvel at that single tree you just painted. Find the brief moments of closure amid the longer periods where it is lacking. Celebrate as you go, rejoicing in the now rather than waiting for the not yet.

LIVING WITH INCOMPLETION

I've listed Incompletion next to the end of the creative tools because it incorporates so many of the others, in particular Re-creation and reframing. Creative people may deal with ambiguity better than others, but we still like clarity and closure when we can get it. Sometimes, however, we won't, at least for a while. This is where reframing, and especially, faith, comes in.

I remember standing in the hospital room next to my wife who was about to go into surgery for breast cancer. All such moments are incomplete. You don't know how the surgery will go, what the results will be, what future chemo treatments will do to you, etc. And in that moment, the nurse told my wife this: "I'm a breast cancer survivor myself and I will tell you what someone told me when I was going into this same surgery: 'An amazing life awaits you on the other side of this.'"

The nurse understood that closure was a very long way off. But she reframed the situation. She gave hope, as well as deep compassion. And that one line helped my wife not just through the surgery, but through the misery of chemotherapy, through radiation treatments, and even to this day as she comes alongside other women with cancer who are now going through the struggle and fear.

In a less dramatic context, that same line applies to us as adventurous creatives. We all reach places where we get stuck or lost. We question why we're even bothering. But as the bumper sticker tells us, "God's not done with me yet." We inhabit Incompletion at such times. But an amazing life still awaits us.

Challenges are inevitable, but the way through them is to know there is something amazing on the other side. The following graph shows a process that is known by different names, one of which is The Emotional Cycle of Change.[68]

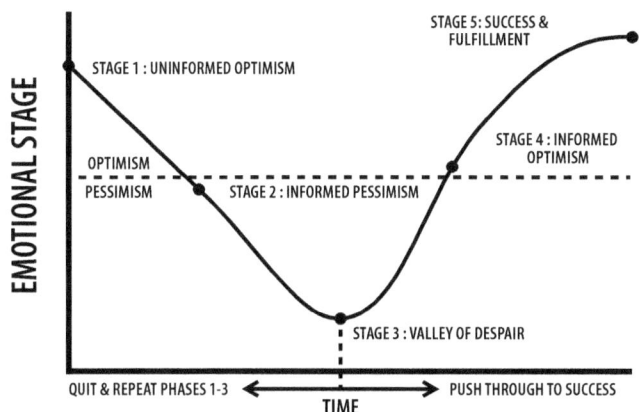

It's a familiar journey for almost any project. You start out enthusiastic (because you do not know how hard it will be). Your emotions slip as you realize what you're up against. And then you hit The Valley of Despair. We all get there, and nobody likes it. In the Valley, you'll either give up (which, let's be real, can be the best option in some cases), or push on to where you understand what is happening and how to bring it all together. And that leads to the final stage that we all crave, "Success & Fulfillment."

At every stage, you'll have moments of Incompletion. And when you feel stuck, you can turn to all the points in Chapter 11 on Movement. But through it all, you can practice a kind of active waiting. Living in Incompletion isn't a hopeless sitting on your hands until some rescue arrives. I see it instead as an anticipatory time of looking forward to what God will pull off and doing what I can now to get there. As the sculptor Auguste Rodin put it, "Patience is also a form of action."

I can abide with Jesus even when he's not providing any hints and nudges. While I'm waiting for this layer of paint to dry, I can draft the underlayer of another painting. When I need some distance from a plot point in a short story, I can go prune our Japanese maple, figure out dinner, or solve a bookkeeping issue. While I'm waiting for an answer in one area, I'm merrily scooting along in another.

Eventually, I get to the final stage of success (which we all love). But before that is my favorite, Stage 4. In it, I reach a point where the work doesn't just feel possible; it feels inevitable. One day, I'm still not sure how it will come together. And the next, I'm certain I'll finish it, but in a way I never considered before this stage. At that moment, I experience a fresh sense of creative momentum.

FREEDOM IN LIMITATIONS

To maintain that momentum through a project or really, through The Creative Wild, I'll often impose limits. That may mean I intentionally leave certain parts of the canvas incomplete or roughly sketched so I can add greater detail to other areas. I can choose to leave out characters in my novel so that the ones that remain have more depth. I can even impose deadlines or other artificial constraints on my process to help me focus and complete the project. It's another example of how leaving some things incomplete is the way you achieve completion.

Limits seem restrictive. We think we want innumerable options. But research shows that an overabundance overwhelms us. In addition, limits force me to improvise. To practice both creativity and ingenuity, that MacGyver-like ability to make things up as I go and use whatever materials present themselves. Such constraints aren't obstacles I work around as a second-best option. They are my doorway to freedom and my primary means of completing a project.

At least, when finishing is my goal…

LETTING OTHERS COMPLETE THE WORK

Sometimes you don't want to complete the work. Not fully. You want to leave things open, hanging. Not for you, but for your audiences. You want them to provide enough closure at the right moments, while also leaving them wanting more. In writing fiction, for example, the writer's ability to build unresolved (for a while) tension keeps the reader turning pages. It's not just devising mini cliffhangers at the end of each chapter. It's giving enough details—the right details—for the reader to fill in what's missing. Leaving enough incomplete gives the reader an insider's sense of both participation and accomplishment. It's like the advice from poet Stanley Kunitz, who says of poetry, "End with an image. Don't explain it."[69]

The same principle applies to the world of visual art as well. In *Art and Illusion*, art historian E. H. Gombrich refers to this act of participation by the audience as "The Beholder's Share."[70] He notes how, throughout history, leaving out elements of art works enhances both the role and the enjoyment of the viewer. Gombrich cites, for example, 16th century painter and biographer, Georgio Vasari's comment that "...all things which are far removed, be they paintings, sculptures, or whatever, have more beauty and greater force when they are a beautiful sketch [una bella bozza] than when they are finished."[71] This trend of leaving elements out continued through to the Impressionists where the viewer had to fill in the blanks to make the scene "read." Or with most contemporary art, how it requires the viewer to bring their own meaning to the work.

In your own creative work, what can you leave out for your audiences to complete? What can you give them that will make them feel like insiders? What little "inside joke" can you share? What experience can you create around the work that gives them greater opportunities for involvement? Engaging your audiences as co-creators gives them a taste of what it feels like to explore, discover, and even make, the same things you feel when you create.

THE VALUE OF LEAVING THINGS OUT

Core to making the experience satisfying for your audiences includes choosing *which* elements to include—or leave out—to improve the overall effect for them.

Artist and writer Kent Nerburn captures this well:

(At) its heart, our art is about what we don't put in—what we considered and rejected; the choices withheld in order to illuminate the choices made. The actor knows the pauses that create tension; the musician knows the rests that build poignancy and offer relief; the novelist knows the spaces in conversations; the painter knows the detail that isn't described... Early in the practice of our art we seldom think of these things. We believe the essence of the art is what is created, not what is left out. But as we get older we discover that it is the absence that takes up the most space, the silence that speaks most loudly and surrounds what is heard with meaning. The goal of any art is to pare down to the essence. The French writer Antoine de Saint-Exupéry said that true art is achieved not when there is nothing more to be added but when nothing more can be taken away.[72]

THE INCOMPLETENESS OF INCOMPLETION

We've seen how most creative work—and life—contains elements of Incompletion. These can frustrate you when you're in the Valley of Despair but exhilarate you when you move beyond it and find micro accomplishments along the way. We also explored why embracing limits leads to freedom and how leaving parts of your work incomplete builds interest and participation from your audiences. There are clear benefits to embracing Incompletion.

But I'm not suggesting it is easy. We will always seek closure. The key is knowing when that's appropriate and when not. For example, if you recall in Chapter 13, Place, I mentioned a time on a flight where, after praying, the words on a page almost popped out to me and provided me with a needed answer to a client project. What I didn't tell you was this:

For months afterwards, I would tell clients and others, whenever they confronted a creative challenge, that "You're only a prayer away from a creative breakthrough." It sounded inspiring. I even believed it at the time. It just doesn't hold up as a rule because it's not universally true.

Think of how many times you've prayed for a breakthrough, and nothing happens. For example, at Christian writers' meetings, I've often heard authors tell their journey to getting published. It's almost always a variation on the same theme: "I finally hit a point where I surrendered everything to Jesus, and then suddenly, I finished my book, had an agent, and got published." After yet another such testimonial, the guy next to me whispered, "Yeah, great. How about all of us who have reached that point of surrender a dozen times and nothing happens?" I knew exactly what he meant.

Desperation can be a necessary factor in recognizing our need for God. If it were the chief contributor to answered prayers, we'd have a handy formula. But remember the point on formulas in the Bible. Just ask anyone who has prayed for lost family, unemployment, or the cure for an illness. All desperate, all in a state of Incompletion, yet no immediate answer to prayer.

One of the most hidden aspects of our creativity is that God is creating something in us we don't see now, something that may differ from what we're seeking. It may be deeply hidden, like Jesus' first thirty years of living in obscurity. But it is always in our best interests even if we can't see it now.

Thus, while I'd love an immediate answer for each creative challenge, I've learned to accept the pause. To live longer in

Incompletion. To wait well. Because as you've likely experienced too, the responses to our prayers, when and how they come, are usually so much better than we expected.

QUESTIONS AND EXPLORATIONS
- How does limiting your options feel to you? When phrased in such general terms, it likely feels restrictive. But reframe the question like this: What could you eliminate from a current project or process that would provide you with greater freedom?
- Mystery and wonder both contain elements of Incompletion. What is the mystery both in and behind your current work? What don't you know about it that might add new depth to it?
- How might you leave part of a current project incomplete so that your audiences could feel a greater sense of accomplishment and participation?

RIGHTNESS: *WOODWORKING*

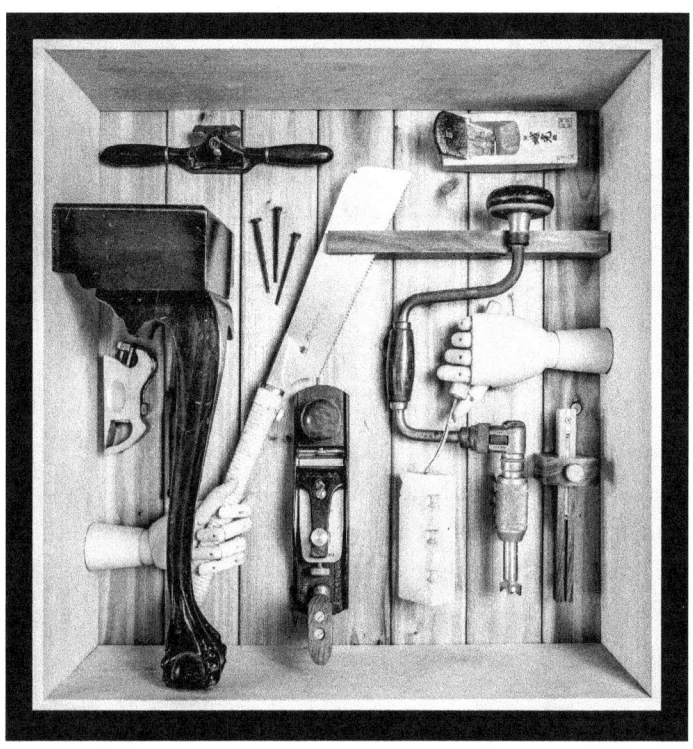

I learned some basics of woodworking from my dad and from a junior high wood shop class. But my skills and interest took off when my wife and I bought our first home, a 1924 Spanish bungalow near Pasadena, California.

We renovated virtually every room in the house. But what made the biggest difference was when I designed and built rocking chairs for my two sons when each was born.

The first chair, a Mission-style rocker, taught me a lot about the complexities of angled joinery that must bear heavy loads. But our second son's rocker took my aspirations and skills to a new level. I got ambitious and designed a wooden rocker with a sculpted wooden seat whose back could recline (much like in a movie theater where the seat slides forward as the back goes down so that you maintain balance on the rockers).

I went through countless prototypes to get the curvature of the back slats comfortable in all positions, but the effort paid off. I can still find design flaws in it (as I can with everything I've made since, from desks to an armoire and entertainment center to bar stools, a bar cart, jewelry boxes, tables, a 3D chess set, trick cabinets that house photos and other collections, kitchen tools, sculptures, and a wealth of other artifacts). But I'm still proud of the efforts.

Each one felt right enough at the time. But as I lived with the piece, I have sensed something isn't quite there. In some cases, I know what it is, say, the thickness of the legs. In others, I can't tell exactly. But I continue to both make and refine my sense of Rightness so that one day, I will make something and think, "Yes. That's it. That feels just right."

Or so I hope.

CHAPTER 17
RIGHTNESS

Where you learn how to know if your work is ready, done, and right.

Don't try to comprehend with your mind. Your minds are very limited. Use your intuition.
— Madeleine L'Engle, *A Wind in the Door*

If you want to annoy a poet, explain his poetry.
— Nassim Nicholas Taleb, ***The Bed of Procrustes: Philosophical and Practical Aphorisms***

A hunch is creativity trying to tell you something.
— Frank Capra

Many consider Chris Bianco to be the best pizza maker in the world. When Chris was young, he trained in a cheese shop in New York with a master of the craft. Chris once asked the man, when they were forming a large batch of mozzarella cheese, "How do you know when the mozzarella is ready?" The man replied, "When it smiles."[73]

I recently met with Chris at the Los Angeles branch of his restaurant, Pizza Bianco. I asked him about the quote. He said that making the mozzarella smile is something you *feel* more than you know. I asked if you can push it too far. He said you can always go too far, as he put it, like trying to make the mozzarella laugh (which he said with a laugh). But knowing when the mozzarella smiles is like knowing the totality of a thing and sensing, not just when it is ready. But when it is right.

So how do you know when your creative work is ready or "right?" I'll tell you three ways. And then I'll explain why none of them is sufficient on their own. Especially this first one.

RELYING ON THE MARKET

The first way to know if your work is ready or right is to let the market decide.

Bad move.

Letting the public decide if your work is ready is like letting your toddler decide what tie you should wear to your job interview. They'll have an opinion, but it won't necessarily help you. It's true that the best validation we have that our work resonates with someone is when they pay money for it. And that the greatest success is someone loving our work so much they tell others. But we can't know either of those ahead of time. We should listen to and try to understand our audiences and build our work around their interests, needs, and even dreams. That's vital to us directing our own interests to areas that may resonate with theirs. You can test with sample products or get feedback from posting examples to social media. Still, you don't know for sure about *this* product, painting, book, business, or other creative effort.

Movie studios test and research all the time. Yet, as screenwriter William Goldman famously pointed out about their inability to pick a hit movie, "Nobody knows anything." In *The Practice,* Seth Godin notes there are three reasons your work doesn't sell. One, it's not the right audience. Two, it's the right audience but the wrong timing. Three, your work or your skills aren't of an acceptable quality for your audience. Good points, but for many of us, they can feel like the old line about the executive who knows that half of his advertising spending is wasted. He just doesn't know which half.

We can't know if others will think our work is good, because there's no common agreement about what that means. In his book, *Fearless Writing*, William Kenower tells about the debut novel from author Erica Bauermeister. Multiple publications reviewed it, including two newspapers:

Newspaper A thought Erica could write good sentences. The review went something like this: The School of Essential Ingredients *is an exciting debut, made all the better by Ms. Bauermeister's ability to turn an appealing phrase. For instance, this gem from the middle of the book: 'The passengers jostled on the train like potatoes boiling in a pot.' Newspaper B gave her book a mixed review:* The School of Essential Ingredients *showed promise, but suffered a bit from Ms. Bauermeister's stilted language. Consider this clunker: 'The passengers jostled on the train like potatoes boiling in a pot.'*[74]

Same sentence, but two different responses from professional reviewers. Kenower continues:

...one of the first things I teach my (writing) students is to never ask themselves, 'I wonder if what I've written is any good?' This is a death question, by which I mean that you will die before you can answer it definitively. Instead, the only two questions a writer should ask are the following: 'What do I want to say?' and 'Have I said it?' If you're asking anything else, you're not writing—you're just worrying.[75]

You may have to modify these two questions for other types of creative work, but the principle remains: The way to know if your work is right doesn't depend on the market. It depends on you. Which leads us to the next approach.

KNOWING WHEN IT IS READY

The second—and best—way for discerning when your work is ready is through your own internal sense of Rightness. I admit, Rightness is a squishy term, much like love or beauty, one that defies definition, but is recognizable when experienced. You've likely felt it. You knew, without testing, when to take the cake from the oven. Or you changed the chorus of the song because, somehow, it just didn't fit the rest of the piece.

It's like the scene from the film *Mr. Turner,* where the artist J.M.W. Turner hangs his painting in the exhibition hall along with the other painters waiting for their works to be judged. He stares at his work, then rushes off, grabs his paints and a brush. To the horror of the other painters around him, he then daubs a splash of bright orange onto the center of the image. No one changes their painting when it is hanging in the salon. Unless, like Turner, you realize it wasn't quite right. And that single stroke transformed an interesting piece into a brilliant work of art.

Rightness is much like what Malcolm Gladwell describes in *Blink,* an intuition or instinct, a level of knowing that transcends our cognitive abilities. Much of it comes through exposure. Like character, the people and influences you invite into your life shape it. To aid that, you can read, absorb, or re-create work people you respect have deemed of good quality. You can even try to understand why others admire works you dislike. It helps to create a set of standards for your medium or project based on your level of experience in that area. These can be principles that have worked for you before that you want to maintain in all you do, or requirements imposed by a client for specific project.

What will also help in cultivating your sense of Rightness is refining your judgment and tastes. I used to confuse those two words, thinking, for example, that I didn't like opera. But what I now realize is that while the subject matter of opera is too melodramatic for my *tastes*, I can appreciate the quality of the music and singing (a matter of judgment). I may not like a particular fashion designer's work (a matter of taste), but I can respect her skill in color usage (a judgment). Understanding the difference helps me be more discerning in both. It also helps me filter the comments from others about my work.

In the end, however, our sense of Rightness will be a combo plate of tastes, judgment, intuition, instincts, and a lot more. It includes the biblical notion of discernment and expands as we seek the wisdom the Bible promises us (James 1:5). But what shapes these and will contribute most to your growth as a creator is your commitment to excellence.

FOCUSING ON EXCELLENCE

As we just saw, your sense of Rightness may differ from someone else's. So how do you navigate a world of subjectivity? Artist Ken Nerburn offers a way:

(If) there is no reliable measure of quality, there is one reliable internal measure that you can still use as a guide. It is excellence. Excellence is a habit—it is a mode of creating. It is fluid and it is malleable in its expression, but it is consistent in its intention. If you establish the habit of excellence in your work, it will always be there, no matter how distant you feel from that work or how flawed it felt in the act of creation. Excellence cannot be quantified and it is different for each person. It is where your character shines through your creation. It is your commitment, frozen in time and space. It is your spiritual signature on your work...The only honourable position of any artist is to be as present as possible to every act of creation and to treat each work as if it is the last they will ever create.[76]

As with standards, context matters. You won't produce the same level of quality in a 30-minute sketch that you will in a painting that takes 30 hours. A minimum-viable-product-level prototype should, in fact, be sloppy or else you're wasting time on the wrong details. But you can still commit to giving your best, given the circumstances, constraints, and resources available to you at the time.

If, however, you let "good enough" be your ongoing standard for everything, you'll diminish more than just your work. Death by a thousand cuts is still death. All those little compromises add up. But keep in mind, this is not about perfectionism. You'll notice I'm bringing this up near the end of this book, not at the beginning. If you obsess about excellence too soon, you'll never get started. You'll let perfectionism squelch your ability to just dive in, make bad first drafts, and create adventurously. If, however, once you're into your project and especially near its end, if you don't focus on excellence, you'll get stuck in the morass of mediocrity. You need an awareness of context, a sense of adventure, and a commitment to excellence, as well as the wisdom about how to apply each. Doing so will help get your work to a place where you sense it is right.

Until that sense fails you.

That usually happens when you need it most, at the end of a project. It occurs because you're too close to the work. You can't tell if it sings or thumps. And that is when you need the third option, others you can trust.

THE VALUE OF THE FEW

This third way to know if your work is ready is to ask those who know you *and* the work well. For my writing, I have a handful of trusted critique partners who will tell me if what I've composed is working for them. And because they are, to varying degrees, members of my audience (e.g. you probably don't want astrophysicist nonfiction critique partners if you're writing Amish Romance), I know that their judgment is attuned to mine. When my sense of Rightness gets lost, I can rely on theirs.

For example, I can count on Rick to provide a big picture perspective. Pat will always note my best sentences, yet also find my weakest sections. Michelle will call me out whenever I'm being less than honest, not just with the reader, but with my heart. Collectively, they point out what works and what doesn't. Whatever their unique contribution, they are people I trust. Which, as Kevin Kelly notes, is an essential element to your creative success: "Three things you need: The ability to not give up something till it works, the ability to give up something that does not work, and the trust in other people to help you distinguish between the two."[77]

Small circles of such trusted advisers can be invaluable. So too can just one person at the right time.

MAINTAINING A COMMITMENT TO EXCELLENCE

While making the Creativity Boxes you've seen between each chapter, my son Connor, a commercial director, helped me tremendously with lighting or suggestions for arrangements. But his greatest value came when I was working on the fourth box, the one on gardening/landscape design. I was content to go with a more floral arrangement. You can see these previous versions at www.ExploreYourWorld.com/creativity-boxes. I felt it was good enough. He pushed back. Hard.

"Why would you do that, Dad?" "You can do better." "If you stop now, anyone could do that." I had a déjà vu moment of my time in China, where my other son said something similar. And then it hit me. I realized I was treating these creativity boxes like a client project. I was getting them to a point of good enough because I was more concerned about getting them done. I was making productivity the highest goal. He was challenging me to see them as works of art.

The worst part of all this was that I knew he was right before he said anything. My internal sense of Rightness had been screaming "Danger, Will Robinson!" even as my productivity-minded self was saying, "Oh, it's fine," hoping no one would notice.

Don't think like that.

Love takes time. Art takes time. Productivity fights against time. We need productivity to keep us moving, to provide helpful deadlines, and to prevent us from spinning. But, in both love and art, we sometimes must give far more than we think we can afford, in hours, effort, and emotions. And we can only do so when we believe the results will be worth it. Not in terms of a payoff or quid pro quo investment mindset. But because this is right. This is why we're on this planet.

WHEN YOUR NEEDS EXCEED YOUR ABILITIES

So there you have it. While the market may not help so much, you can still know if your creative work is ready through your own sense of Rightness and from trusted advisers.

But what if they say your work isn't ready? And what if you agree? The obvious answer is, you improve it. But what if you don't know how?

Well, you can keep at it until you do. Ernest Hemingway admitted to writing 39 endings to *A Farewell to Arms* before he landed on the one he felt was right.[78] Thus, you can always play Dory and "just keep swimming" until you get there. But what if you don't know if you have it in you to do that? That's a scary proposition.

It's where you reach a point when not knowing the way forward shifts from "What do I do now?" to "What if I can't?" That's a whole new level of impostor syndrome.

Take this chapter you're reading, for example. I'm currently on the 11th version of it. With each revision, I thought I was getting closer to something right, even as the result never quite felt that way. I sensed a fuller story but couldn't convey what it was.

One Sunday morning before church, I read the most recent version to my wife. I was hoping she'd express an enthusiasm that I wasn't quite feeling myself. No such luck. "You're not showing up in it," she said. "Arghhh!" I wanted to cry out, to lash out. But I knew she was right.

At that point, I felt a mix of despair and frustration: I had no idea how to fix this or what to do—except to pray in desperation. I was out of answers. And out of time. We had to get to church.

Remember how "where you are affects who you are?" Going to church unknotted some of the anxiety of not knowing. But it also shifted my horizons. By getting away from home and from writing, even for a few hours, I realized this chapter wasn't the totality of my existence. Then, during the service, things shifted even more. I sensed God's presence in a way I hadn't for weeks. Amid singing songs of praise *to* God, I received a powerful gift *from* God.

I had gone seeking answers to a problem in my writing. He responded with an outpouring of grace for a problem in my soul. And as only God can do, his touch there in church turned out to be the answer to both. Sounds like that moment in the therapist's office, doesn't it?

I remember very little of the sermon that followed. Instead, I couldn't keep up with what I was sensing from God about this chapter and my relationship with him and how the two were more intertwined than I realized. Here's the gist:

You may have noticed in this book that I can go for large sections on each chapter without mentioning God. Usually, that's because I see God in everything I do, so I don't feel a need to mention him in every paragraph. But in this chapter, it was the same symptom, but a different root issue. Here, it reflects how I was writing this. I was so head-down-nose-to-the-ground racing forward that I'd stopped abiding with Jesus. Yes, I prayed and kinda sorta invited him into the work. But there comes a point where both God and I know when I'm faking it. I wasn't aware of how little I was giving of myself to God until I realized how little I had to give to the writing. Until I hit the wall.

On that Sunday morning, God's first response wasn't, "Oh, it's about time" or even, "Just write this!" Instead, he reminded me of his deep love, concern, grace, and presence. He knew I had lost my way relationally as much as creatively. He cares about my work. But he cares more about me and you.

Then came the more surprising response.

Instead of a breakthrough idea, he provided me with a kind of divine reframing. He reminded me I'm a creative adventurer. That I can do what any good adventurer does. I can pivot and find another path. That I have this entire tool kit of adventurous creativity tools. That when I feel like I am at the end of my abilities, I can re-create what I've done differently. Reframe it. Seek an indirect approach. Choose to leave certain areas incomplete to provide greater clarity to the ones that I include. Here I was thinking I was stuck and had nothing left, that the pantry was all empty. Then he shows me he's got supermarkets full of stuff. Cattle on a thousand hills and all that. All available to me. And not just as tips and techniques, but through his Spirit, as a *supernatural* means of moving forward.

For writers and other creatives, God often hides what he wants us to say—or in this case, what he wants us to first discover—until we realize we cannot figure it out on our own. He's not a mean instructor withholding the prize until we get the right answer. He's the loving parent waiting for us to see the gift he's placed before us, but we've been too caught up in our own thing to realize. He waits until we are ready.

At the core of this was remembering how much I needed him. Him. God. Not just the answer to my current crisis. He's not my magic genie. My desperate plea for help didn't trigger an alarm in heaven like the Bat Phone, where now I'd surrendered enough to warrant a response. It didn't change God. It changed me.

I cannot explain how this all works. I'm nervous even telling you of how God answered me, as if all this came through clearly articulated words. Prayer, for me, doesn't operate that way. But then, neither does Rightness. There are ways of knowing that go beyond words. There are mysteries too big for explanations. Do I understand literally what it means for mozzarella to smile? Or when a work is "right," or how God answers prayers or speaks to us? I do not. Not in ways I can explain. Yet still, *I know*. Even if sometimes I forget.

We need our own instincts and standards, refined over time. We need others to help us shape our work and make it ready for the fickleness of the market. But most of all, we need God. Both as audience and as co-creator. To be a part of all we do.

From this point, I can't control whether you, the reader, will resonate with any of this. But I do know that this draft differs from the dozen that came before because now, for the first time, it feels as right as I can, on this day in this place, make it. I will run it by my trusted advisers and test it with my audience. I will continue to pray. All so that this chapter does more than feels ready. I will push until, hopefully, it—and really, this entire book you have now read—smiles.

QUESTIONS AND EXPLORATIONS
- Try to find three works of art or literature that others have deemed great but that you don't like. Just go online and search for "most famous works of art" or the same for literature and you'll have plenty of choices. Then, make a case for why each of the three is "good."
- Rightness also applies to how you choose what to work on. Try this. Make a list of all the creative projects you could do. Assign a number from 1 to 10, with 1 being not excited and 10 for those that you can't wait to work on. Now cross off everything that isn't a 9-10. Seriously. Your gut tells you what's most important. Everything else is a distraction.
- To know when a work is done, rely on deadlines (the creative's inconvenient savior), accountability to others, and stopping when adding anything more detracts. What else helps you finish?

CHAPTER 18
NEXT STEPS

Where you learn what to do with what you've learned.

Be not afraid of going slowly, be afraid only of standing still.
— **Chinese Proverb**

God doesn't always give us a blueprint for our lives, but he always gives us a next step.
— **Joyce Meyer**

You've reached the end of *The Creative Wild*, the book. Now it is time for you to dive into or re-enter The Creative Wild itself. Still, you may have a head full of wonderings and a heart full of desire, and you're not sure what to do with all that you've just learned. Here are some next steps you can consider.

PRAY, REFLECT, THEN DO

Ask God to show you what he'd have you do. Seems obvious. But herein lies one of our biggest challenges as creative believers. When we get excited by a new idea or project, we tend to ignore everything else because those moments of clarity don't come all that often. So when we have them, we want to run with them. But even in your excitement to get started, take time to abide and listen. Not as a killjoy, but to invite God into your idea or project. When I do this, I don't throttle back my enthusiasm. I double it.

So take a moment right now and invite God into your reflection. Then ask, "What ideas stood out to me or attracted me most?" They may not be ideas for a new project, so much as how to incorporate something you've learned here into your existing creative practice. See what happens.

A variation on this is to ask, "What am I most inspired to *do* now?" A horrible habit of mine is to read some book, say on watercolors, and get all inspired and then do nothing. Too often, I'd rather dream about creating than to create. Dreaming is fine, but now is the time to do. What has this book inspired you to attempt?

For example, my editor, Deb, someone for whom you'd have thought this was just another work project, said this, "As I was reading (your book) and when I was finished, I wanted to get out in the garden and plant flowers, whip out my watercolors and sketchbook and draw, and start playing the piano again... which I haven't done in years (it's in the basement and out of tune)." You don't have to attempt a masterpiece or a massive undertaking. Start small and simple. But start. And consider something handmade. There's a magic to connecting in a tactile way that will further inspire you to keep creating even more.

My wife, Kris, recently noted something similar. She works in a knitting store and has told me of so many people who come there wanting to learn to knit simply because they want to make something with their hands. In a world of screens and the increasing use of AI, they are discovering, as Kris put it, "how good it feels for your soul when you're using your hands." So if there is anything you've ever wanted to make, particularly with your hands, don't put it off.

CHOOSE YOUR TOOL

Now, regarding all the creative tools covered in the previous chapters, don't try to apply them all at once. If you do, you'll either need more caffeine than the human body can tolerate, you'll get overwhelmed, or you'll burn out. Thus, I suggest you tackle one, or only a few, tools at a time. As I've noted repeatedly, go with what interests you. If you're realizing your studio or that corner of the bedroom where you write could use a facelift, go for it. Make your creative space inspiring. Or perhaps you're intrigued by the notion of your creative assets. Catalog those and consider ones you don't have but might like to add. If you feel you've been running dry on ideas, turn to the exercises in Chapter 15, Indirection, to increase your output. You get the idea. Or you will.

Creating is hard work. But having the right tools makes that work go smoother. It's like woodworking. Planing an entire tabletop smooth with a hand plane will always raise a sweat. But using a sharp plane with the right technique will be a rewarding joy. Trying to plane against the grain with a dull plane iron (the blade part) will raise both your sweat and your blood pressure. You may see that plane fly—across your shop as you heave it in frustration.

I still think that the idea of flow is rather magical, as well as paradoxical: The harder the work—the more it captivates you while challenging you—the more you lose yourself in it and enjoy it. It's an empirical experience that helps me understand why taking up Jesus's yoke (Matthew 11:28-30) can be a positive thing and not just hard labor. There is sheer joy and a sense of accomplishment and purpose in doing hard things you love that overcomes—or really, transforms—the effort.

So find your favorite creative tool. Take it out for a spin. Use it enough to understand its potential. Then try another. Then another. Your goal is to familiarize yourself with them so you can apply them when needed. You may not need one for some time, but knowing how to use it means you know when to turn to it when you do. Remember that subtle point about what makes a person successful creatively? They need mastery, motivation, mindset, and a supportive environment. But within mindset is that critical element of understanding the creative process and these corresponding creative tools. Without knowing various creativity tools and techniques, mastery of your medium will only get you so far. For example, a painter who doesn't know how to generate fresh ideas may be technically brilliant, but her work will probably not grow or resonate in the way it could.

To aid you in using these tools for creating adventurously, you can find what I call The Creative Wild Questions in the Appendix. It's a version of what I use in my branding work. It takes each tool and gives you a set of questions you can use to apply that tool to a project. I encourage you not only to try some of them to get to know the tools better, but to come up with your own questions you can use. Keep yourself and your tools sharp.

LET YOUR CREATIVITY ENHANCE YOUR FAITH

Back in the Introduction, I noted one reason for writing this book was to understand better how our faith affects our creativity and vice versa. We've explored the first part of that with the ideas of inviting Jesus into our joy, abiding with him as we make, and seeing creating as an act of grace. But I want to end with a few thoughts on the "…and vice versa" part.

A few years ago, my colleagues and I did a project for a major Christian ministry. Our goal was to develop an initiative that would help believers to get unstuck when they felt spiritually dry. I applied much of what you've read here to that project since I've been rather obsessed with these ideas for years, but never found the right venue in which to convey them. In sharing what I'd been thinking about with others, I found that we'd all had a common experience in the Church.

Whenever one of us was feeling distant from God and asked for advice, the usual answers were:
- read your Bible more,

- pray more,
- confess your sins,
- fellowship with others, and
- worship.

That's about it. There weren't a lot of alternative suggestions.

Prayer, bible reading, and the other points are essential. But there's more to our spiritual lives than that, more of the incarnational, experiential element.

We're each wired to respond to God in different ways. Some may find that getting out in nature is a balm to their soul. Others reignite their passion for God through music. Or, it could be making a meal or sharing it with others, reading good literature, watching films, reading poetry, playing games, or doing any form of creative work. Whatever the case, you and I will likely have different spiritual wirings and triggers in what connects us to God.

Here's the connection back to our topic at hand: Figuring all that out is a highly creative process.

Just recognizing that we're all different in what gets us unstuck spiritually or leads us to praise is the first step. Determining what that is and then doing something about it is the next. I may know that music can get me out of a funk and reorient my longings back to God. But if I'm not creative in what music I select or when I choose to listen, I won't gain the full benefit. If nature is my special way of reconnecting with God, just going outside can help. But what aids me even more is making an adventure of it and going some place new, a location where the awe of nature leads to an awe of its Creator. In short, the more creative I am in leveraging my spiritual wiring, the more I reconnect in powerful ways when I've drifted or feel spiritually stale.

Another way to connect your creativity to your faith is to take what you've learned about abiding with Jesus in your creative work and apply it to all of life. As I noted earlier, I've found it's easier for me to abide when I'm making something because

I'm usually in a better mood than when, say, dealing with a difficult relationship situation or being bored on a long drive. But what I've discovered is this: I will *feel* differently in those other situations, but I can still seek God's presence. It all comes down to faith: Do I believe God is with me and listening and caring, even when I don't sense that?

I used to think of "faith" as the cop out answer whenever I didn't have a more concrete explanation. Now, I see faith—much like grace—for the gift that it is. Not just a gift God gives us that makes it possible for us to believe in this invisible being we call God, but a gift in the sense of something I can rest in. Creating adventurously and abiding with Jesus as I do so has taught me just how much God is always there, always supportive, always seeking my best. It's like the phrase I overuse: Get to, not have to. I *get to* rely on faith for the mysteries I will never figure out rather than I *have to* accept something on faith because I don't have any better option.

In a similar vein, my creative life has helped my faith life in terms of a more lived-experience approach to grace and paradox. The "both/and" theme that runs through this book regarding creativity has spilled over into other areas of my life as well. When confronted with what seems like an either/or choice, I can now reject the false dichotomy and look for the best of both sides of the situation. It makes me far more tolerant of others because I know there's more than meets the eye to an angry response from a stranger or a caustic remark from a friend. In a culture that increasingly dehumanizes and demonizes those with whom we disagree, this both/and approach enables you and me to be bridge builders.

As we previously saw, we stand in the space between secular culture and that of the Church. There will be times when we must speak the truth in love boldly and clearly. But our ability to live with ambiguity, seek and extend grace, pursue a both/and perspective, and find analogies and artistic expressions rather than arguments helps us be ambassadors for Christ. Both inside and outside the Church.

Finally, at least in terms of how creativity affects our faith, I've a much greater tolerance now for the messiness of making. Not just making art or creative work for clients, but making anything: a meal, a family, a neighborhood, a friend, a life. Embracing a life of adventurous creativity has taught me so much about grace in all its form, from overcoming perfectionism to accepting the humanity of others—and myself.

And in that spirit of messy making, I encourage you to take a mini retreat. A few hours if you can, or even a few minutes. But get alone with God and jot down your own list of how your creativity has affected or is affecting your faith and relationship with Jesus. And if it all feels highly aspirational, no worries. Make it your dream list of how you'd like to live. It's messy, right? So, as with creativity itself, there's no wrong way to do this other than to not try.

GET MORE CREATIVE WILD RESOURCES

Now, if all of what you've read inspires a desire for more, I've got you covered. In the following pages, you'll find:

- **The Creative Wild Questions.** You can think of this as a summary of the book, but its value is in turning the key points of each chapter into a set of questions to ask yourself as you're creating. It's a simple way to apply each of the tools to any project.
- **The endnotes and bibliographical references.** You'll find the quote sources and references here, but you can see a far more extensive bibliography on the website.
- **Acknowledgements.** I'll never be able to thank all the people in my life who have influenced me creatively, but this is a list of a few who have directly helped me with this book.

And speaking of the website, I've noted throughout the book various additional resources at ExploreYourWorlds.com (don't forget the "s" in "worlds"). Here's a list of all that is there currently but I'll be adding more over time:

- **A more detailed list on how to create adventurously**. This expands on the list in Chapter 3 and can remind you of who you are as an adventurous creative.
- **Reasons people don't consider themselves creative** (and how to change that). If you've struggled with the label of artist or creative, this will help convince you that you belong in The Creative Wild.
- **Extended bibliography.** This lists around 250 of the resources used in the writing of this book. There were hundreds more, but the ones here were what I found to be the most useful.
- **More ways to get unstuck**. This is a detailed list of exercises and techniques to try when you're stuck that expands on those in the chapter on Movement.
- **Creating in grace manifesto**. This is my list of what life might look like if I truly created as an act of grace. Use it to inspire you to release fear and abide with God more as you create.
- **What motivates me.** This is my list of both what motivates me to create, and also what de-motivates me. It also contains a long list of ways to get more inspired to make something.
- **The Value of Incompletion**: Yet another list, this time showing additional ways that Incompletion can aid in your creative work.
- **The making of the Creativity Boxes.** This is a behind-the-scenes review of how I made many of the Creativity Boxes you've seen between the previous chapters.
- **Bonus Chapter: Abide and Create.** This extra chapter expands on aspects of Chapters 1 and 2 and explores more about what it means to abide with Jesus as you create.

That's it for now. I hope you've both enjoyed and have gained something of use from this journey through *The Creative Wild*. Most of all, I hope this book has inspired and equipped you, as an adventurous creative, to do the one thing you were put on this planet to do.

Just make something.

Use this QR code as an easy way to access these and other Creative Wild resources. Or just use this link:
www.ExploreYourWorlds.com/Creative-Wild

APPENDIX: THE CREATIVE WILD QUESTIONS

The following takes the creative tools you've just learned about and turns them into a set of questions. It's a helpful review of some of the key topics, but most of all, a useful tool for creating adventurously. Ask yourself these questions at the start of a project or whenever you feel stuck creatively.

PART I AND II CONCEPTS
- How could I be more adventurous in the making of this project?
- How might I abide more with Jesus in it? What would it look like to intentionally invite him into the joy of making this?
- What can I do to remind myself, right now, that I am creative? That creating is good? That God both loves and delights in me?
- What can I do to stay in the Flow Zone?
- In what ways can I practice more wisely?
- How can I pursue what most excites me right now creatively? What is that specifically? In what medium?
- What rules or advice am I following that may not be helpful? What would a better approach be?
- What limiting beliefs do I need to work on to reframe them into something more in line with how God sees me?
- What can I do to re-engage my deep longing and childhood joy in creating?
- How does this work represent the right (to me) balance of ideology and imagination? What is that right balance?

READINESS
- What am I most interested in right now?
- What other assets do I have that I could apply to this?
- How can I use the change management formula in Chapter 7 to identify the variables that I need to work on here?
- What baby step or bad first draft could I make right now to overcome perfectionism and get me moving?

RHYTHM
- How could a change of pace help here? Am I rushing when I should slow down and vice versa?
- What systems can I put in place to help me create no matter my mood?
- What work am I in the mood to do now?
- What activity fits that mood?
- In what ways can I better "love my work like an amateur and do my work like a pro?"

RE-CREATION
- How could I refine this to make it better?
- Where or who could I turn to in a different field, to either inspire or inform me?
- What techniques would help me most here?
- What might this look like in a different medium or format? Which one excites me the most?
- How could I experiment my way into a new idea?

DISCOVERY
- How could I use my other senses, either to solve the problem or to create something more inviting for my audience?
- What can I discover here that's new and interesting that I haven't noticed before?
- What Easter egg or detail can I help my audience discover?

- Have I reviewed all my notes and sparks recently to see if there's something hidden I've overlooked?
- How and when might I do a creative God Hunt?

MOVEMENT

- What would lead to momentum for this project?
- How can I see this setback or frustration as traction and thus helpful?
- In what area would working a bit harder (and smarter) make the biggest difference?
- When I start to feel stuck, which tactic from the list in the chapter (or on the website) seems the best fit to get me moving again?
- What's a simple next step I can take to move me further on this project?
- Am I taking time daily for minimum creative doses?
- How can I order my time to allow deep dives?

PERSPECTIVE

- How can I reframe this (project, situation, career stage)?
- What are five other ways to perceive this same situation, idea, or creative product?
- What might this look like from a variety of different perspectives (a child's, a specific audience member, someone in the press, if I didn't care about what people thought, etc.)?
- How does this work reflect my voice and style? How could I get more of myself into it?
- What does success look like for this specific project?

PLACE

- Where could I go that would inspire me or bring a minor disruption to my day/project?

- What environment is most conducive to this day and stage of the project?
- What new place could I try that might help?
- What environmental factors (light, sound, temperature, other people, etc.) could I test to see what works best for me for different projects or phases in a project?
- Where can I go for safety and security to create in peace?
- Where might I go for disruption or to be adventurously challenged creatively?

OTHERS

- How could others help me? For ideas? For input? For services or techniques they do better than me?
- How could I create an experience of delight for others with this?
- How can I bless others and who can I bless with this?
- Who can talk me off the ledge or remind me of my first love?
- Have I taken time to be alone with God and leave all this with him? How could I do that more right now?

INDIRECTION

- How might I take an indirect approach to this? What would that look like?
- What are three alternative approaches to this idea or project? Five? Ten? Fifty?
- What would this project look like in a different context, format, channel, or medium, and what could I learn from that?
- Have I identified the root problem or just a symptom? What is the root issue?
- How could I apply Beginner's Mind to this situation?

INCOMPLETION

- What can/should I leave incomplete at this moment?
- What, right now, should I say "no" to?

- How can I trust God to complete this? What would that look like?
- How can I add elements of Incompletion to my work for my audience to complete?
- In what area of my creative life do I feel most incomplete? How can I better invite God into that area?
- What can I eliminate from this work that will strengthen it?

RIGHTNESS
- Am I basing my sense of rightness for this project on judgment or taste or my intuition? What previous projects confirm that my instincts here are trustworthy?
- What do trusted voices tell me about whether this is ready or right?
- How might I celebrate this work—and the process of making it—more?
- How have I listened to my audiences without letting them direct my creative decisions? What do I know about their felt needs and dreams related to this kind of creative work?
- What could I do to listen to what God says about this work, and if it is ready?

ENDNOTES

1. Wiman, Christian, *My Bright Abyss*, Farrar, Straus and Giroux (April 2, 2013), Kindle version Loc. 1344-48
2. Buechner, Frederick, *Wishful Thinking: A Seeker's ABC*, HarperOne; Expanded edition (September 24, 1993)
3. Lamott, Anne, as found in Barron, Carrie and Barron, Alton, *The Creativity Cure: A Do-It-Yourself Prescription for Happiness*, Scribner (August 6, 2013), Kindle version Location 520-21
4. https://en.wikipedia.org/wiki/Adventure
5. Burkus, David, *The Myths of Creativity: The Truth About How Innovative Companies and People Generate Great Ideas*, Jossey-Bass; 1st edition (October 7, 2013), Location131-67
6. Patchett, Ann, *This Is the Story of a Happy Marriage*, Harper; Reprint edition (November 5, 2013), Location 430-37
7. Greene, Robert, *Mastery*, Penguin Books; Reprint edition (October 29, 2013)
8. Robinson, Ken, *Out of Our Minds: The Power of Being Creative*, Capstone; 3rd edition (November 13, 2017), p. 163
9. Johnson, Steven, *The Innovator's Cookbook: Essentials for Inventing What Is Next*, Riverhead Books; Illustrated edition (October 4, 2011), Highlight Loc. 525-32
10. Barton, Ruth Haley, *Sacred Rhythms: Arranging Our Lives for Spiritual Transformation*, IVP; Annotated edition (February 10, 2006), p. 27
11. Robinson, Ken, *Out of Our Minds: The Power of Being Creative*, Capstone; 3rd edition (November 13, 2017), p. 163
12. Henry, Todd, Louder than Words: *Harness the Power of Your Authentic Voice*, Portfolio (August 11, 2015), Location 537-539
13. Mueller, Jennifer, *Creative Change: Why We Resist It . . . How We Can Embrace It*, Harper Business; Reprint edition (January 2, 2018), p. 63

14 Ashton, Kevin, *How to Fly a Horse: The Secret History of Creation, Invention, and Discovery,* Anchor (January 20, 2015), Location 1368-76
15 Whelchel, Hugh, "More Than Just a Bus Ticket: The Four-Chapter Gospel (Part 3)", February 16, 2012, https://tifwe.org/more-than-just-a-bus-ticket-the-four-chapter-gospel-part-3/
16 Ashton, Kevin, *How to Fly a Horse: The Secret History of Creation, Invention, and Discovery,* Anchor (January 20, 2015), Location *1378-80*
17 Csikszentmihalyi, Mihaly, Creativity: *Flow and the Psychology of Discovery and Invention (Harper Perennial Modern Classics)*, HarperCollins e-books; 1st edition (October 13, 2009)
18 Wolfe, Gregory, *Beauty Will Save the World: Recovering the Human in an Ideological Age,* Intercollegiate Studies Institute; First Edition (June 15, 2011), p. 24.
19 Fujimura, Makoto, *Art and Faith: A Theology of Making*, Yale University Press; First Edition (January 5, 2021), p. 5
20 Wiman, Christian, *My Bright Abyss,* Farrar, Straus and Giroux (April 2, 2013), Location 1759-62
21 Koberg, Don; Bagnall, Jim, *The Universal Traveler: A Soft-Systems Guide to: Creativity, Problem-Solving, and the Process of Reaching Goals,* W. Kaufmann; Revised edition (January 1, 1974)
22 Penn, Joanna, *The Creative Penn Podcast*, interview with Becca Simes, September 6, 2021 at https://www.thecreativepenn.com/2021/09/06/strengths-for-writers/
23 *Kenower, William. Fearless Writing: How to Create Boldly and Write with Confidence, Penguin Publishing Group. Kindle Edition, pp. 53-54*
24 *L'Engle, Madeleine, Walking on Water: Reflections on Faith and Art, Convergent Books (October 11, 2016),* Location *970-75*
25 O'Donohue, John, *Beauty: The Invisible Embrace,* Harper Perennial; Reprint edition (March 1, 2005) p. 6

26 Issacson, Walter, *Leonardo da Vinci*, Simon & Schuster; Unabridged edition (October 2, 2018), Location 1334-1351

27 Bayles, David; Orland, Ted, *Art & Fear: Observations on the Perils (and Rewards) of Artmaking*, Image Continuum Press; 1st edition (April 1, 2001), Location 350-55

28 Brinkhoff, Tim, "Why Arthur Schopenhauer thought music was the greatest of all art forms," https://bigthink.com/high-culture/schopenhauer-music-will/

29 Csikszentmihalyi, Mihaly, *Flow: The Psychology of Optimal Experience (Harper Perennial Modern Classics)* 1st Edition, Kindle Edition, HarperCollins e-books; 1st edition (August 18, 2008)

30 Godin, Seth, *The Practice: Shipping Creative Work*, Portfolio (November 3, 2020)

31 Story told to me by Jeff Lind with supporting research from Townend, Richard, "Walking to Fame: Bach's Visit to Buxtehude," https://www.gresham.ac.uk/watch-now/walking-fame-bachs-visit-buxtehude)

32 Peterson, Andrew, *Adorning the Dark: Thoughts on Community, Calling, and the Mystery of Making*, B&H Books (October 15, 2019), Location 520-27

33 Kleon, Austin, *Steal Like an Artist: 10 Things Nobody Told You About Being Creative*, Workman Publishing Company; 1st edition (February 28, 2012), p. 35

34 Johann Wolfgang von Goethe as quoted in Long, Pricilla, *Minding the Muse: A Handbook for Painters, Composers, Writers, and Other Creators*, Coffeetown Press (June 24, 2016), Location 330-32

35 Bayles, David; Orland, Ted, *Art & Fear: Observations on the Perils (and Rewards) of Artmaking*, Image Continuum Press; 1st edition (April 1, 2001), Location 339-47

36 Brothers, Cammy, Michelangelo, *Drawing, and the Invention of Architecture*, Yale University Press; First Edition (September 23, 2008)

37 Robert Cormier, author of *After the First Death* found in *Martin, Paul Raymond, Inspiration & Motivation: Writer's Little Instruction Book,* Writer's Digest Books, Cincinnati, OH, 2005, p. 173
38 Brock, Stephen W., *Hidden Travel,* Sublimity Press, 2021, p. 170
39 Kleon, Austin, *Keep Going: 10 Ways to Stay Creative in Good Times and Bad,* Workman Publishing Company; Illustrated edition (April 2, 2019), p 32
40 *Florence in Detail* by Claudio Gatti as quoted in *Kerper, Barrie, Paris: The Collected Traveler (Vintage Departures),* Vintage; Reprint edition (July 12, 2011), Location 145-153
41 Thompson, Derek, "Hot Streaks in Your Career Don't Happen by Accident", *The Atlantic,* https://www.theatlantic.com/ideas/archive/2021/11/hot-streaks-in-your-career-dont-happen-by-accident/620514/
42 Buchman, Lorne M., *Make to Know: From Spaces of Uncertainty to Creative Discovery*, Thames & Hudson (October 12, 2021), Location 849
43 Staton, Tyler, *Praying Like Monks, Living Like Fools*, Zondervan Books (October 4, 2022)
44 Kaufman, Scott Barry, and Gregoire, Carolyn, *Wired to Create: Unraveling the Mysteries of the Creative Mind*, TarcherPerigee (December 29, 2015), Location 1622-23
45 Ashton, Kevin, *How to Fly a Horse: The Secret History of Creation, Invention, and Discovery,* Anchor (January 20, 2015), Location 470-84
46 Ashton, Kevin, *How to Fly a Horse: The Secret History of Creation, Invention, and Discovery,* Anchor (January 20, 2015), Location 2751-55
47 Martin, Paul Raymond, *Inspiration & Motivation: Writer's Little Instruction Book*, Writer's Digest Books, Cincinnati, OH, 2005, p. 87

48 Paul, Annie Murphy, "The Benefits of "Creative Grit," https://anniemurphypaul.substack.com/p/the-benefits-of-creative-grit?-publication_id=396126&post_id=113300534&triggerSave=true

49 Kadavy, David, *Mind Management, Not Time Management: Productivity When Creativity Matters (Getting Art Done Book 2)*, Kadavy, Inc. (October 15, 2020), pp. 184-185

50 Iyer, Pico, *The Art of Stillness: Adventures in Going Nowhere*, Simon & Schuster/ TED (November 4, 2014), Location 123-31

51 Holiday, Ryan, "The Most Successful People Are The Ones You've Never Heard Of (And Why They Want It That Way)," https://medium.com/the-mission/the-most-successful-people-are-the-ones-youve-never-heard-of-and-why-they-want-it-that-way-5a25d92186fd

52 Garcia, Hector, *The Magic of Japan*, Tuttle Publishing (September 14, 2021), p. 38

53 Brock, Stephen W., *Hidden Travel*, Sublimity Press, 2021, p. 40

54 Adams, James L., *Conceptual Blockbusting: A Guide to Better Ideas, Fifth Edition*, Basic Books; 5th edition (September 3, 2019), Location 1380-91

55 Paul, Annie Murphy, "Why You Should Be Task-Switching More Often," https://anniemurphypaul.substack.com/p/why-you-should-be-task-switching

56 Rattner, Donald, *My Creative Space: How to Design Your Home to Stimulate Ideas and Spark Innovation*, Skyhorse; Illustrated edition (October 15, 2019)

57 Inspired by points in Brown, Pauline, *Aesthetic Intelligence: How to Boost It and Use It in Business and Beyond*, Harper Business (November 26, 2019), p. 161

58 Brooks, David, *The Social Animal: The Hidden Sources of Love, Character, and Achievement*, Random House Trade Paperbacks; Reprint edition (January 3, 2012), Location 4372-87

59 Henry, Todd, *The Accidental Creative: How to Be Brilliant at a Moment's Notice*, Portfolio (August 27, 2013), Location 1288-90

60 Dillard, Annie, *The Writing Life*, Harper Perennial (November 12, 2013)
61 Ashton, Kevin, *How to Fly a Horse: The Secret History of Creation, Invention, and Discovery*, Anchor (January 20, 2015), Location 3612-19
62 Dodson, Bert, *Keys to Drawing with the Imagination*, North Light Books; Kindle edition (June 28, 2017), Location 109-15
63 Brynteson, Richard, *Innovation at Work: 55 Activities to Spark Your Team's Creativity*, AMACOM, September 5, 2012
64 Kelly, Kevin, "The Technium: 103 Bits of Advice I Wish I Had Known," https://kk.org/thetechnium/103-bits-of-advice-i-wish-i-had-known/
65 Barker, Eric, "Barking Up The Wrong Tree" enewsletter, September 6th, 2021
66 Carson, Shelley. *Your Creative Brain (Harvard Health Publications)*,Wiley, Kindle Edition, pp. 77-78
67 Berger, Warren, *CAD Monkeys, Dinosaur Babies, and T-Shaped People: Inside the World of Design Thinking and How It Can Spark Creativity and Innovation*, Penguin Books; Kindleedition (December 28, 2010), Location 415-21
68 Five Stages You Move Through Emotionally When Changing Behavior | InFocus Leadership Solutions, https://www.infocusleadership.ca/blog/five-stages-move-emotionally-changing-behavior/
69 Pádraig Ó Tuama on Benjamin Gucciardi's work *The Rungs*, https://onbeing.org/programs/benjamin-gucciardi-the-rungs/
70 Gombrich, E. H., *Art and Illusion*, Princeton University Press; 2nd edition (March 21, 1969), p. 191
71 Gombrich, E. H., *Art and Illusion*, Princeton University Press; 2nd edition (March 21, 1969), p. 193
72 Nerburn, Kent. *The Artist's Journey, On Making Art & Being an Artist*, Canongate Books. Kindle Edition, pp. 77-78

73 Netflix, "Chef's Table Pizza" episode with Chris Bianco
74 Kenower, William. *Fearless Writing: How to Create Boldly and Write with Confidence,* Penguin Publishing Group. Kindle Edition, pp. 52-53
75 Kenower, William, *Fearless Writing: How to Create Boldly and Write with Confidence,* Penguin Publishing Group. Kindle Edition, p. 53
76 Nerburn, Kent, T*he Artist's Journey: On Making Art & Being an Artist,* Canongate Books; Main edition (November 24, 2020), p. 34
77 Kelly, Kevin, "The Technium: 103 Bits of Advice I Wish I Had Known," https://kk.org/thetechnium/103-bits-of-advice-i-wish-i-had-known/
78 Hemingway, Patrick in the forward to Hemingway, Ernest, *A Moveable Feast: The Restored Edition,* Scribner (January 1, 1994)

You can find the full bibliography with almost two hundred additional references at ExploreYourWorlds.com/Creative-Wild/Bibliography. Or just use this handy QR code.

ACKNOWLEDGMENTS

Writing acknowledgments for a book like this is like being asked which of your friends—or worse, your kids—is your favorite. It's impossible to say anything other than, "All of them." For that's how I feel about all the people who have helped me on my creative journey. They are also too numerous and diverse to name individually here.

So let me extend a blanket thank you to the broader list of artists, writers, and other creatives who have inspired me, those who have taught me, those with whom I've worked or served (that means you, all you wonderful clients), and anyone else who has engaged with me in some creative effort, I will focus here on those who have helped specifically with this book. And even that isn't complete for there are so many of you that I have interviewed in a casual way and whose ideas get expressed here in general statements such as "artists I know" or "creatives who do this" and the like. Please forgive me if I've not mentioned you here. It's not out of a lack of appreciation as much as a lack of space and adequate short-term memory.

Thus, to make this even simpler (for me, and less painful for you to keep reading all my caveats), I will stick with those who I call out in the book or whose ideas I have used, and those who have contributed directly as readers of various early drafts. The former includes Chris Bianco, Byron Borger, Jenae Cartright, Al Erisman, Jack Fortin, Jeff Goins, Sister Laura, Jeff and Teresa Lind, Matt Mikalatos, Cody Miller, Charlie Peacock, Joanna Penn, Brian Rayburn, Andy and Lauren Shurson, and Dave Waller.

The latter includes my beta readers Rhoda Bangerter, Laura Cox, Caroline DePalatis, Kay Edwards, Colleen Hicks, Jana Holdrege, Karen Koch, Lidia Lae, Sara Marlin, and Jef Miller. And finally, my editor Deb Beddoe and my invaluable critique partners Rick Rosenkranz and Pat Schantz, along with Michelle

Mays who has been with me on this writing journey for over 15 years and has helped in ways beyond writing.

Next, there's family including my parents, Lonnie and Marilyn Brock, and my favorite (yes, we both know they are my only ones as well) in-laws, Stan and Esther Belland, as well as my brother-in-law, Eric Belland. Then we get to the inside team, my sons Sumner (the painter and graphic designer) and Connor (the commercial director and woodworker) who have contributed to this book in more ways than they realize or that I can count.

And then, there's my wife, Kris. I know it is almost a cliche to say, "I couldn't have done this without her," but it is true. Without her support and encouragement for over 35 years, I wouldn't have been able to commit the time and focus to creative pursuits, nor would I have had the desire to do so. I can only say "thank you" and look forward to what God is doing with her on her own creative journey.

Finally, there's the Alpha and Omega, the beginning and end of my every creative thought, longing, and work. With the Father, Son, and Holy Spirit, there is a way of creating and making that, as we've seen with grace, is too good to be true. But it is. And for that, I am eternally grateful.

Wait. Are you still here? C'mon. Go out and make something!

But if you just can't decide on what to do next, consider these:

- Review this book on your favorite online bookstore or book review site. I can't guarantee that a great review will gain you God's favor, but it would mine (insert happy face emoji here so we're clear on the intended humor).
- Go to ExploreYourWorlds.com/Creative-Wild and dive into the free resources (or use this QR code):

- Tell God how grateful you are for the ability to create.
- Then tell your family and friends how grateful you are for each of them.
- Then go make something. Go on.

www.ingramcontent.com/pod-product-compliance
Lightning Source LLC
Chambersburg PA
CBHW052137070526
44585CB00017B/1870